GERHARD
VON RAD

Makers of the Modern Theological Mind

Bob E. Patterson, Editor

Makers of the Modern Theological Mind

Bob E. Patterson, Editor

GERHARD VON RAD

by James L. Crenshaw

HENDRICKSON
PUBLISHERS
PEABODY, MASSACHUSETTS 01961-3473

GERHARD VON RAD

Copyright © 1978
Hendrickson Publishers, Inc.
P.O. Box 3473
Peabody, Massachusetts 01961-3473
All rights reserved.
Printed in the United States of America

ISBN 0-943575-69-9

Library of Congress Cataloging-in-Publication Data

Crenshaw, James L.
    Gerhard von Rad / by James L. Crenshaw.
        p. cm.
    Reprint. Originally published: Waco, Tex.: Word Books,
c1978. (Makers of the modern theological mind).
    Includes bibliographical references.
    ISBN 0-943575-69-9
    1. Rad, Gerhard von, 1901-1971   I. Title. II. Series:
Makers of the modern theological mind.
[BS1161.R3C73 1991]
221'.092-dc20   90-28697
                                                              CIP

To David

Contents

Editor's Preface

Who are the thinkers that have shaped Christian theology in our time? This series tries to answer that question by providing a reliable guide to the ideas of the men who have significantly charted the theological seas of our century. In the current revival of theology, these books will give a new generation the opportunity to be exposed to significant minds. They are not meant, however, to be a substitute for a careful study of the original works of these makers of the modern theological mind.

This series is not for the lazy. Each major theologian is examined carefully and critically—his life, his theological method, his most germinal ideas, his weaknesses as a thinker, his place in the theological spectrum, and his chief contribution to the climate of theology today. The books are written with the assumption that laymen will read them and enter into the theological dialogue that is so necessary to the church as a whole. At the same time they are carefully enough designed to give assurance to a Ph.D. student in theology preparing for his preliminary exams.

Each author in the series is a professional scholar and theologian in his own right. All are specialists on, and in some cases have studied with, the theologians about whom they write. Welcome to the series.

Bob E. Patterson, Editor
Baylor University

Foreword

One greets this book with the warmest welcome. It introduces a scholar who, in this century, has surely been one of the world's most influential theologians, and it will be useful both for those well-acquainted with Gerhard von Rad and for those who do not know his work. It is apparent that Professor Crenshaw is engaged in a fascinating dialogue with von Rad. The reader will find a portrait of a unique personality which was in its essence shaped entirely by his intimate study and knowledge of the biblical texts.

James L. Crenshaw has especially investigated von Rad's entire literary corpus with great care. With sensitivity he has presented von Rad's methodology and approach as well as his artistic achievement, knowing that von Rad's interpretation of Old Testament texts enables one to see them with new insight. Thus the author draws his readers into a fresh confrontation with the Old and then the New Testaments. In this book one finds a continuation of von Rad's unique gift for making the Old Testament exciting for several generations of university students in all fields, students of theology, and pastors.

But the book also has significance for the history of Old Testament research, for this discussion of von Rad's work goes beyond biographical interests. Here the results of von Rad's work are not only appropriately presented but critically examined. Crenshaw's own studies find expression, and he discusses the work of many others, some who contradicted von Rad's views during his lifetime, and some who only in recent years have offered opposing interpretations. Gerhard von Rad's contribution will become even more clear in the scholarly discussion of the second half of this century.

Gerhard von Rad was buried in the cemetery of Heidelberg-Handschuhsheim. A plaque at his grave, in addition to giving his name and dates of birth and death, pictures the prophet Jonah being released from the fish—a symbol of the resurrection drawn from the Old Testament.

May this book contribute to a new perception of the Bible's witness to the resurrection, in the service of which stood the life and work of Gerhard von Rad.

HANS WALTER WOLFF

Heidelberg, November 1977

Preface

This book was conceived more than six years ago, when I agreed to contribute what was then envisioned as the final volume to the series, Makers of the Modern Theological Mind. It seemed appropriate that at least one specialist in Old Testament studies appear in that list of significant thinkers, for the name Gerhard von Rad belonged alongside those of Rudolf Bultmann, Paul Tillich, Martin Buber, Karl Barth, and others. I fervently hope this analysis of von Rad's thought will commend his works to beginning students and ministers for whom this series is intended, but that it will also open up new insights for those who know his writings well.

During the academic year 1972–73, I was privileged to study at the University of Heidelberg on sabbatical. There I met Mrs. Luise von Rad, who graciously talked with me on more than one occasion, and I became thoroughly acquainted with the setting in which her husband worked from 1949 until his death in 1971. This experience in Heidelberg also gave me an opportunity to meet von Rad's successor, Hans Walter Wolff, who assisted me greatly in gaining access to the rich library resources available to me that year. At his invitation, I attended the memorial service at which addresses were given by Wolff, Rolf Rendtorff, and Wolfhart Pannenberg.

In the ensuing years at Vanderbilt University I have fashioned the positions within this book by testing them upon students, particularly in a seminar on von Rad's thought, but also in courses dealing with methodological problems and exegesis. Two persons, Toni Craven and Nicole Garel, read the manuscript and offered helpful suggestions, for which I am most appreciative. I wish also to thank Hans Walter Wolff for kindly agreeing to write a foreword for this volume, and Gary Stansell of Saint Olaf College, Northfield, Minnesota, for translating his mentor's remarks into English. Finally, the University Research Council at Vanderbilt generously awarded me a summer stipend to complete the writing of this book. The Council's continuing support of my research has been a constant source of encouragement.

This volume is dedicated to our youngest son, David. My wife joins me in thanking him for the immeasurable joy he brings to our household, and in wishing that he will move freely in the traditions we cherish until he discovers the silence of God which evokes constant dialogue with eternity.

JAMES L. CRENSHAW
April 18, 1978

I. The Little Historical Monoman

LIFE AND INFLUENCE

A recent publication bears the title, "Old Testament Theology before and after Gerhard von Rad." [1] Such a title gives witness to the unique contribution of one man to the course of Old Testament theology. Whatever one may think about the program inaugurated by von Rad and carried through with a brilliance hardly matched in the brief history of his particular discipline (and the response has been especially vigorous, both positive and negative [2]), it must be admitted that the influence of this man marks a decisive stage in the history of Old Testament theology. For von Rad's approach also did much to erase the earlier distinction between Old Testament introduction and theology. Thus his influence has been keenly felt throughout the broad discipline of Old Testament studies. It would be difficult to find an Old Testament scholar anywhere who is not indebted to Gerhard von Rad in one way or another. In this way he has taken up the torch previously borne by his countrymen Julius

16   GERHARD VON RAD

Wellhausen (1844–1918) and Hermann Gunkel (1862–1932).

Julius Wellhausen's extraordinary gifts had enabled him to refine and make credible to the scholarly community the documentary hypothesis of four literary sources resting behind the Pentateuch. These consisted of the Yahwist (J), the Elohist (E), the Deuteronomist (D), and the Priestly source (P). The designations for the first two were derived from the divine name they seem to have preferred, Yahweh and Elohim respectively. Although the Priestly source also employed the divine name Elohim, decisive differences within the texts using this general word for God led to distinguishing two distinct sources on the basis of content. The Elohist had a discernible northern bias, told of visions and angels, and emphasized the fear of God. The Priestly source was dull and repetitious; it treated ritual at length, and had a fondness for genealogy. The four sources arose during the interval between the ninth and fifth centuries.

Historical interests prompted Wellhausen to write a synthesis of the history of Israel which was published in the *Encyclopaedia Britannica* and became the standard work on the subject.[3] He believed the prophetic age represented the apex of Old Testament religion, a high point flanked both before and after by lower religious forms, primitive religion and priestly religion. His radical views eventually led to the State's refusal to grant him the privilege of teaching the Old Testament, and resulted in his shift into New Testament studies and eventually into Arabic studies, where he made a considerable contribution to the discipline. Largely due to his work in the Old Testament, the name Wellhausen has become synonymous with the documentary hypothesis of JEDP as literary sources of the Pentateuch.

Hermann Gunkel's impact upon Old Testament studies came at quite another place. He penetrated behind literary sources to an oral stage of transmission, seeking to identify and characterize the different forms of speech and to recognize their function in the daily life of the people. His approach was closely related to the research on fairy tales being undertaken at that time by the Grimm brothers, and contained strong affinities with the history of religions school. Gunkel searched for the life-situation of literary forms, believing that form and content were appropriate to function. His pioneer works in Genesis and Psalms stand as indispensable contributions to Old Testament studies.

The term "form criticism" has been applied to Gunkel's approach. According to it, one searches for specific literary forms, traces the history of those types, and places them within their life setting. For example, according to Gunkel, Genesis abounds in cultic sagas justifying Yahweh worship at a particular sanctuary, or etiological narratives explaining some unusual historical, geographical, or social phenomenon. Genealogical sagas, blessings, treaties, and ethnic origins fill the stories of Genesis. Gunkel attempted to understand the original function of these separate oral forms, and to trace their literary history. In Psalms, he recognized various types: individual complaint and collective lament, hymn, royal psalm, and wisdom psalm. In general, one can say that Gunkel sought to understand the function of a given literary form within the Israelite community.

In summary, one could say that Wellhausen focused upon literary sources that comprise the books Genesis through Deuteronomy, whereas Gunkel moved further back to an oral stage that preceded the written text. For Wellhausen, written sources from different eras underlay the Pentateuch, while Gunkel emphasized the long period of oral transmission when competing accounts met various spiritual needs of the people. The composition was decisive for Wellhausen; Gunkel downplayed the importance of the actual writing down of such traditions. Form critics followed Gunkel in recognizing the manifold use to which

various traditions were put within the Israelite cult. The Pentateuch was a living tradition, acting upon the lives of the people
and being transformed in the process. Both literary criticism and
form criticism tended to isolate individual units within the
Pentateuch, and consequently placed its unity in question.

To both Wellhausen and Gunkel, von Rad owed a great debt.
But he endeavored to recapture the thematic unity of larger
textual units. One can discern decisive shifts and breakthroughs
within his thought during the course of his literary career, to
which I now turn.

The life of Gerhard von Rad was far from ordinary, in spite
of his claims to the contrary ("the normal life of a university
professor runs quietly and without external sensations").[4] Born
into a patrician medical family of Nürnberg on October 21,
1901, von Rad had an early interest in classical philology.
Nevertheless he came under the powerful influence of the Word
as proclaimed by a local minister, Wilhelm Stählin, and by a
young schoolteacher whose name has been forgotten but the
impact of whose teachings has survived in von Rad himself.
Consequently, when von Rad began to cast his eyes around in
search of a profession, he chose to enter theological studies. His
initial interests at Erlangen and Tübingen were not in Old
Testament; in fact, it is reported that Paul Volz, who is perhaps
best known for his studies on Israelite eschatology, and Otto
Procksch, who wrote a valuable commentary on Genesis and to
whom Walter Eichrodt is indebted for the general structure of
his Old Testament theology, made less of an impression on him
than did E. F. K. Müller's lectures on John, and the systematic
theologians Karl Heim and Paul Althaus. Both Heim and
Althaus gathered a considerable following, particularly among
the more conservative members of the German church. After
completing his theological studies in 1925, von Rad accepted a
position as pastor in the Bavarian national church. At this time

he had no intention of entering the ranks of the scholarly community; however, his daily struggle with a growing anti-Semitism prompted the young pastor to request a leave of absence to return to theological studies in quest of an answer to the problem posed to the Christian church by the Old Testament.

Although Otto Procksch supervised von Rad's dissertation, *The People of God in Deuteronomy*,[5] the book owes much to the friendly counsel of Albrecht Alt (1883–1956) at Leipzig. Alt is best remembered for an essay on Israelite law, in which he distinguished apodictic (categorical, absolute, as in "Thou shalt . . . ") and casuistic law (conditional, as in "If a man steals . . . then he shall . . . "). Essentially, Alt was interested in Israelite history, on which subject he published widely. Upon completion of his dissertation, von Rad faced a difficult decision: whether to return to the pastorate or enter the teaching profession; both doors stood wide open for him. Despite the strong advice of a friend, Karl Nold,[6] to leave the university for the more challenging pastoral role, the appeal of university life prevailed upon him. Leonhard Rost, who wrote an important analysis of the story about the succession to the Davidic throne (2 Sam. 9–20, 1 Kings 1–2), departed from Erlangen to Berlin, leaving an opening that von Rad's mentor, Procksch, quickly secured for him.

Meanwhile the young scholar completed his book on *The Concept of History in the Work of the Chronicler*,[7] and availed himself of the opportunity to study further with Alt, whose seminar in the Book of Zechariah led von Rad to tackle Semitic studies in order to keep up with Alt's wide ranging interests. It did not take Alt long, however, to recognize that the chief interest of the young teacher was theological rather than historical. Von Rad thus complemented Alt's approach to the Old Testament. It is not surprising that in 1930 Alt invited him to teach at Leipzig. At the same time an invitation was extended to him

to become the pastor of a Bavarian church. The choice was not
an easy one. Von Rad's vital interest in promoting the well-
being of the church can be seen in everything he wrote. Clearly,
he found it difficult to turn his back upon an opportunity to work
toward the nurturing of souls. Despite his desire to have von Rad
accept the position at Leipzig, Alt wisely recognized that the
decision was wholly von Rad's and refrained from putting pres-
sure on him.

The warm relationship between the two men even at this time
stands out in a letter from Alt to von Rad which has been published by Hans Walter Wolff, von Rad's successor at Heidelberg.[8] Alt assured von Rad that he did not want to infringe on
his freedom to make up his own mind, but wished to assist him
in reaching an informed decision. He went on to answer a fundamental question von Rad had written about: academic or prac-
tical profession. Alt told him that if having tried academia he
found it wanting, he could readily change to the ministry. The
other issue he discussed concerns von Rad's actual responsibili-
ties at Leipzig, particularly in archeological excavations and
philology. Alt freely offered his assistance in helping von Rad
achieve competence. Finally, he informed von Rad of a forth-
coming trip to Nürnberg and told him he would gladly meet him
for an hour at the train station.

This friendship deepened with von Rad's decision to move
to Leipzig in 1930. The next four years were busy ones in which
von Rad prepared himself for participation with Alt in archeological work in Palestine. From this period came his essays "The
Tent and the Ark," "There Remains Still a Rest for the People
of God: An Investigation of a Biblical Conception," "The False
Prophets," [9] and "The Priestly Writing in the Hexateuch." [10]

In 1934, Willy Staerk, who wrote the first major commentary
on Psalms using Gunkel's method, extended an invitation to von
Rad to move to Jena, where national socialism flourished. Ac-

cepting the challenge, perhaps because of his genuine love for the Hebrew tradition, von Rad soon found that an Old Testament scholar was not welcome in such an environment. He reminded everyone of the Jewish problem by the very fact that he taught the language and literature of ancient Israel. His classes virtually empty, von Rad went in search of hearers, and the following years saw him engaging in seemingly endless illegal church discussions with those who had not surrendered to the anti-Semitism of the day. The bodily risk was great, both from the authorities who had forbidden such conferences and from his extensive travel during the war. Nevertheless, von Rad found in the church a freedom that was not afforded him in the university; here he could speak his mind, confident of a hearing. His contribution to the church was quickly recognized, and led to an offer to become the chief pastor at Hamburg. Choosing rather to remain at Jena, where the task of confronting anti-Semitism was more pronounced, von Rad worked diligently and published prolifically. During these years many popular works in defense of the Old Testament appeared, such as *The Old Testament—God's Word for the Germans!* and *Moses.* But from this period also came the epoch-making programmatic essay, "The Form Critical Problem of the Hexateuch," as well as such important articles as "Notes on the Royal Psalms," "The Beginnings of Historical Writing in Ancient Israel," "The Promised Land and Yahweh's Land in the Hexateuch," and "The Basic Problems of a Biblical Theology of the Old Testament." [11]

THE LITTLE HISTORICAL CREDO

With publication of "The Form Critical Problem of the Hexateuch," von Rad joined the front ranks of Old Testament interpreters. In this essay he set forth the unique approach that has come to be associated with his name. Von Rad believed that a

single confessional statement concerning God's marvelous deeds
in Israel's behalf was recited in various cultic settings and
underwent constant revision according to the experiences
through which the people passed. In time the cultic background
gave way, and confessional statements were freed for use in
many different contexts. In a word, historical traditions arose
and were retold from generation to generation.

In this view, a brief historical credo constitutes the Hexateuch
in miniature. From this confession, the first six books of the
Bible grew as Israel told her story about God's wondrous action
in history. The core tradition concerned the deliverance from
Egypt and subsequent occupation of the promised land. For
this reason, it was called the settlement tradition. Existing in
three forms (Deut. 26:5b–9; 6:20–24; Josh. 24:2b–13), the
settlement tradition underwent free adaptation in various cult
lyrics (1 Sam. 12:8; Ps. 136; Exod. 15; Pss. 105; 78; 135),
until it was finally embellished with elements of the Sinai tradition (Neh. 9:6 ff.; Ps. 106). The separate traditions, settlement and Sinai, testify to redemptive history and divine justice
respectively.

In the historical creed preserved at Deuteronomy 26:5b–9,
von Rad saw a confession of saving facts which grateful Israelites recited in connection with the Feast of Weeks at Gilgal:

A wandering Aramean was my father; and he went down into
Egypt and sojourned there, few in number; and there he became
a nation, great, mighty, and populous. And the Egyptians treated
us harshly, and afflicted us, and laid upon us hard bondage. Then
we cried to the Lord the God of our fathers, and the Lord heard
our voice, and saw our affliction, our toil, and our oppression;
and the Lord brought us out of Egypt with a mighty hand and an
outstretched arm, with great terror, with signs and wonders; and
he brought us into this place and gave us this land, a land flowing with milk and honey.

Here the simple act of returning firstfruits to the Lord became an occasion for a rehearsal of God's wondrous redemptive deeds.

Similarly, the natural inquisitiveness of children concerning the divine statutes imposed upon Israel provided an opportunity for parents to remind their youngsters that Israel once endured bondage to Pharaoh, but that the Lord brought her out of Egypt, with marvelous signs and wonders, and planted her in the land he had sworn to give the fathers (Deut. 6:20–24).

The covenant renewal ceremony recorded in Joshua 24 furnished an occasion for historical retrospect (vv. 2–13). This account of redemptive activity focuses upon the patriarchs, Egyptian bondage, deliverance from captivity, the years of wandering, and the settlement in the land of promise. This Hexateuch in miniature alludes to a considerable body of material concerning the various traditions comprising Genesis 12 through Joshua, with one glaring exception: the Sinai tradition. Von Rad found this gap all the more puzzling because of curious incidentals that are recorded in Joshua 24:2–13 (the miracle of the Reed Sea, the story of Balaam), where one expects an economy of detail but encounters mention of an obedient hornet that drove the inhabitants of the promised land from their dwelling place.

Noting that these three creeds occur in different settings, von Rad distinguished between a constant element, the historical credo, and a variable element, the form of external expression. In the former, he saw the "enumeration of the saving facts which were the constitutive element of the religious community." [12] The cultic form and setting suggested to von Rad that solemn recital must have been an invariable feature of the ancient Israelite cult, whether as a creedal statement or as a hortatory address.

The credo's silence concerning Sinai struck von Rad as par-

ticularly important. In his opinion, the Sinai tradition celebrated God's *coming* to his people, while the settlement tradition
testified to his *guidance* and *redemptive action*. The former
pointed to divine justice, and emphasized apodictic (unconditional) law. The exodus tradition, on the other hand, lauded
divine grace.

If von Rad joined the front ranks of Old Testament scholarship with the publication of this theory about the origins of the
Hexateuch, he proved that he belonged there permanently with
the appearance in 1944 of his essay "The Beginnings of Historical Writing in Ancient Israel." One can scarcely imagine a
more sensitive analysis of a literary text. Here von Rad demonstrated his unusual ability to hear what a biblical text had to say
in ancient Israel. For anyone who has read this masterful essay,
the story will never be the same again.

From the summer of 1944 until June of the following year,
von Rad learned the rigors of war, having been pressed into
military service. In the middle of March he began a confinement
at Bad Kreusnach as a POW that was to last until the end of
June, although the effects of malnutrition continued for years.
Even in such straits von Rad found those who would learn from
him, and displayed a true teacher's concern for his young theologians and pastors. These prisoners of war were the first to
profit from von Rad's understanding of the Book of Genesis,
which he expounded to them daily.

Some fifteen years after this imprisonment, von Rad wrote
down his reflections upon the experience, which his wife has
recently published.[13] Here one finds a vivid account of the last
hours before he was captured, the initial confinement, the constant struggle to stay dry and warm while exposed to the elements by day and night, the ever present hunger, the attempts
at humor and debate, the friendships which developed under
such adverse circumstances, the spiritual ministry von Rad pro-

vided for younger theologians, the gradual easing of his lot and his ultimate release. In addition, a letter written by Walter Fürsts to Mrs. von Rad describes a memorable celebration of the Lord's Supper that lasted more than twenty hours because of the host of people involved, and mentions a sermon by von Rad on the book of Jonah, one by Ernst Käsemann on Paul's teaching about spiritual gifts, and one by Fürsts on Mark 6.

After the war von Rad taught briefly at Bethel, Bonn, and Erlangen, before moving to Göttingen, where the lecture halls were filled to overflowing, in sharp contrast to the two or three students in his classes during his earlier stay at Jena. From this hour of his glory came *Studies in Deuteronomy* and the first fasicle of *Genesis*.

In 1949 he moved to Heidelberg, where he taught until his retirement in 1967. His fame drew students from all parts of the globe; they came to experience theology in the making, and were not disappointed. M. E. Andrew has described these years in a moving tribute to von Rad.[14] He writes that von Rad's early lectures drew about five hundred students in the main auditorium. Even his seminars had as many as a hundred participants. Andrew characterizes von Rad's lectures as often vigorous and original in combination; however, the great mentor gave very little guidance on dissertations. Generous to a fault, von Rad lent books freely and lost valuable works—he did not even own a copy of his own work *The Problem of the Hexateuch*. His colleagues included Edmund Schlink, a systematic theologian and ecumenist; Heinrich Bornkamm, a specialist in Luther; his brother Gunther Bornkamm, a New Testament scholar; and Hans von Campenhausen, a church historian.

From the pen of this Heidelberg Old Testament professor came his classic *Old Testament Theology* in two volumes, *Der Heilige Krieg im alten Israel* (Holy War in Ancient Israel), *Genesis*, *Deuteronomy*, *Wisdom in Israel*, *Das Opfer des Abra-*

ham (The Sacrifice of Abraham), and much more.[15] With his wife's help he busied himself with correcting the proofs of the last-mentioned book on the evening before his death, October 31, 1971.

The academic community was not slow in recognizing von Rad's contribution to its ongoing cause. Five honorary degrees were conferred upon him by the universities of Leipzig, Glasgow, Lund, Wales, and Utrecht. He was selected for membership in the Heidelberg Academy of Sciences, and in 1963 he became the first German Protestant theologian since Adolf von Harnack (author of the standard history of dogma, and best known for his popular *The Essence of Christianity*) to be named to the *Order pour le merité* for Science and Art.[16] Especially popular in the United States and England, particularly among the moderate conservatives, von Rad was chosen for honorary membership in both the Society of Biblical Literature and the Society of Old Testament Studies. His great popularity led in 1960–61 to a semester as visiting professor at Princeton Theological Seminary, and even after his retirement he continued to lecture as health permitted. In the light of these extraordinary feats, it is not surprising that two Festschrifts have appeared in his honor: *Studien zur Theologie der alttestamentlichen Überlieferungen* (Studies on the Theology of Old Testament Traditions) and the massive *Probleme biblischer Theologie* (Problems of Biblical Theology), as well as a memorial volume *Gerhard von Rad: Seine Bedeutung für die Theologie* (Gerhard von Rad: His Significance for Theology).[17]

VON RAD'S ASSESSMENT OF HIS WORK

Among von Rad's many writings stand two brief self-interpretations, occasions in which the mature scholar reflects upon his academic career.[18] In his acceptance speech before the Heidelberg Academy of Sciences, von Rad spoke of the good that he had been privileged to enjoy and the evil that he had resisted. Among the former were his family heritage—that is, the fact that he belonged to the Augsburg patrician class whose conservative nature taught him an appreciation for tradition, and his apprenticeship with Albrecht Alt, his great "teacher" and devoted friend, whose mantle he voluntarily donned and whose spirit he imbibed.[19] The evil that he sought to overcome was the excessive atomization of Old Testament scholarship, the fact that literary critics and historians of religion were failing to show any interest in the larger text, which they were breaking down into its individual units with great skill. For instance, more than twenty literary sources were "discovered" within Genesis alone, and Gunkel's isolation of literary forms called attention to the fragmented character of the book without endeavoring to examine the work in its final form. Confident that the Old Testament was composed of traditions whose history was traceable by means of the form critical method developed by Gunkel, von Rad devoted himself to this task with great diligence and astonishing success. The conviction that the Old Testament itself, rather than systematic theologians, should dictate the form of an Old Testament theology, led von Rad to his great "discovery" of creedal statements which were later expanded into the Hexateuch. In his view, such historical confessions were not limited to the Hexateuch; von Rad hoped that the elucidation of these confessions of faith in Yahweh's decisive action in history would give a depth dimension to Old Testament studies and thus serve as a corrective of the aforementioned atomization.

Elsewhere von Rad defined his task as a university professor as a reading to learn and a reading to teach. This reading was guided by the assumption that there is a radical difference between ancient thought forms and those with which we moderns

operate, a point that von Rad never grew tired of making. Furthermore, his reading sought to correct the then prevalent practice of focusing upon the isolated unit instead of the final form
of the larger text. Von Rad was convinced that the individual
text must come to the aid of the exegete in interpreting the whole
unit; he had no sympathy for the "easy" solution to the problem
of biblical interpretation, namely pneumatic or spiritual exegesis that drew its categories from the New Testament. On the
basis of his constant reading of the text, in which he gave himself wholly in the service of the Word, von Rad discovered a
unique thing in ancient Israel: her necessity to formulate ever
new self-interpretations in the light of God's action in history.
To the elucidation of the full meaning and history of these confessions of faith in divine leadership von Rad devoted his life.
It is significant that in this context of self-analysis, von Rad
mentioned the difficult struggle with national socialism as one
of those unheralded deeds performed by a professor whose inner
life is by necessity concealed from the university community,
but an act nevertheless that preserved something valuable for
posterity. The reflection on his career, too, gives more than a
hint of the struggle with a more powerful enemy, i.e., death's
approaching night.[20]

FUNDAMENTAL THESES

Von Rad's brief pastoral experience shaped an interest that
flourished to the end—a desire to engage in dialogue with the
text of the Scriptures. The devotional interest surfaces again and
again, for von Rad brought to the text an attentive ear. It has
been said that he preferred a powerful heretical sermon to a
powerless one with correct dogma, so convinced was he that the
text must not be divested of its power to address man in his
present circumstances. He preached regularly in St. Peter's

Church at Heidelberg; his next to last sermon there in January 1968 has been seen as symbolic of his legacy to the university.[21] With the campus torn apart by ideological differences, Marxist and Social Democrat, von Rad preached on Joshua 5:13–15, the divine messenger's appearance to Joshua and the falsest of all questions, "Are you for me or against me?" Von Rad reminded his hearers of a greater claim to allegiance, that of the God who sent the messenger. His published sermons are a veritable treasure trove of biblical preaching; it is small wonder that von Rad's daughter edited a collection of his sermon meditations and published them after her father's death,[22] for this dimension of his work cannot be viewed as trivial. Indeed, Wolff writes that in the last years of von Rad's life there was a decisive shift to the moment of meditation.[23] Perhaps the observation of Karl Rahner comes closest to explaining this shift to meditation; Rahner writes that as a reward for faithful service to the text von Rad was led to the Mystery, the Silence of God.[24]

In this eulogy of von Rad, the renowned Roman Catholic theologian who had himself written on *Encounters with Silence* accepts von Rad's self-description of his task in reading to learn and reading to teach, but Rahner points out that the Old Testament scholar *brought something to the text*. One cannot read far in von Rad's works without discovering the truth of Rahner's claim; von Rad was a prodiguous reader,[25] choosing wisely among the treasures of German literature. His interest in Goethe and Thomas Mann enriched the discussions of Job and Joseph, and his love of art resulted in the engaging study of Rembrandt's depictions of the offering of Isaac, which von Rad prefers to call the offering of Abraham. Whether the discipline be anthropology, psychology, semantics, philosophy, or cultural history, von Rad made himself at home as one who reads to learn and reads to teach. In his own field the influence of Gunkel and Alt was decisive, while the works of André Jolles and J. G. von

Herder left their mark upon him in an impressive manner.[26] Jolles wrote in the area of folklore; his book on simple or elemental forms is a masterpiece of rare insight couched in exquisite form. Herder, too, appreciated literature for its aesthetic dimensions. His pioneer analysis of the spirit of Hebrew poetry remains a classic in the field. The combination of von Rad's reverence for the biblical text, a thorough familiarity with the great works of art and literature, and an inquisitive mind led to the creation of matchless prose whose beauty has been said to possess the power to lull the scholar's critical capacity to sleep.[27] No one who has read his works can fail to admire the sheer beauty of expression, nor can he escape the wondrous power of the prose. The reader who is not on occasion moved to tears by the workings of von Rad's mind and the witness to Transcendence must have a heart of stone.

Yet this master stylist was seldom satisfied with his work; he recognized his own limitations. The completion of a manuscript, according to Wolff,[28] was an occasion of sadness in that his reach always exceeded his grasp. Furthermore, the editing of a work for a new edition was especially trying; von Rad likened it to the biblical proverb of a dog returning to its own vomit or a fool repeating his folly (Prov. 26:11). He also protested that his works belong to a certain impasse in German Old Testament scholarship, by which he meant the controversy over the proper way to write theology, and pleaded for that fact to be taken into consideration by readers of his translated works.[29] Nevertheless, he recognized that much of what he wrote was folly, and made changes when preparing some works for new editions. This was particularly the case with the great commentary on Genesis. In short, von Rad responded to his critics by altering his views whenever necessary, although one must admit that the changes were usually minor ones.[30]

While he possessed a marvelous sense of his own shortcomings and is said to have seen in the honor shown him spiritual enrichment and demand, at the same time he was capable of asserting his full authority in professorial fashion. When attacked rather sharply by the New Testament scholar Hans Conzelmann [31] (whose study of the theology of Luke made quite an impact on gospel criticism) for his view of the Old Testament as grace rather than law, von Rad concluded his equally acerbic reply with the warning that the entire Old Testament stood on his side against Conzelmann.[32] Genuine pride occasionally raised its head with von Rad, especially in regard to certain discoveries, for instance that onomastica (noun lists of natural phenomena) rest behind Job 38 and related passages.[33] By demonstrating the presence of noun lists in the Old Testament, von Rad gave plausibility to Alt's theory that Solomon had composed onomastica in verse form. Thus it was possible to view the tradition that Solomon composed three thousand proverbs and a thousand and five songs (1 Kings 4:32; 5:12, Heb. text) as a reliable one.

Von Rad once described himself as a little historical monoman.[34] By this he meant that his constant concern was focused upon the history of Israelite traditions, which von Rad understood as salvation history, that is, confessional statements of divine action. Secular history, or what really happened as understood by the tools of modern critical historians, constituted for him a problem from the very beginning. This issue was never fully resolved,[35] and consequently led to frequent attempts to deal with the difference between saving and secular history. In the end von Rad admitted that his own theology was indeed a phenomenology of Israelite religion,[36] and granted that the task of Old Testament theology was as yet an unfinished one. In essence, von Rad describes Israel's confessional statements, which is a descriptive rather than a theological task. No analysis of faith statements constitutes an explication of faith itself.

It is ironic that von Rad's penultimate book, *Wisdom in Israel*, departs from the traditio-historical methodology that von Rad had perfected and warns Old Testament scholars that there is a very real danger of forgetting the isolated text in favor of the greater whole! [37] Thus we see von Rad return in a sense to the dominant position that existed when he entered the field, namely the focusing of attention upon the tiny unit at the expense of the larger context (von Rad would have said "in the service of the depth dimension of the whole"). It cannot be said, therefore, that von Rad was wedded to a methodology; he even admitted that the perfection of our theology was in danger of doing us in, [38] by which he meant that theological refinement threatened to stifle divine freedom. The result was a remarkable openness to a different approach when the material demanded it; such a change, he felt, was necessitated by Israel's wisdom literature, which constituted a different kind of Yahwism.

But there is a sense in which von Rad never escaped the charge of atomization, as the British Old Testament scholar Norman Porteous has recognized. [39] The fault is not so much von Rad's as it is attributable to the traditio-historical approach that he perfected with consummate skill. Form criticism and tradition history tend to excessive atomization, especially in the insistence that units be considered in complete isolation from other pericopes that would have accompanied the unit under consideration and would have enriched it immensely in the worship of ancient Israel. Porteous singles out von Rad's insistence that the exodus traditions were wholly independent of the Sinai traditions, [40] a conclusion which the evidence by no means demands. But one could multiply such examples easily; in this respect the thesis that every pericope is complete unto itself and contains the full claim to truth—a conviction that arises from an existential stance in approaching scripture and is often heard from adherents of form criticism—has tended to sanction such atomization of the text. Into this pitfall von Rad seldom fell, for he recognized the danger of claiming too much for the biblical text. Indeed, he admits that one can at best trace the footprints of God in the text, and that we can never be sure that the person responsible for preserving the ancient traditions (the traditor) has been faithful to the divine word, or even that the prophet has dealt faithfully with the word vouchsafed to him.[41]

Von Rad's fear of a rational system was deep-seated. Fundamentally it grew out of the fact that a systematic interpretation forced upon the text an artificial strait jacket and robbed it of its freedom to address modern readers in all its power. Such categories as God, man, sin, salvation, and eschatology—the usual divisions of Old Testament theologies—derive from the contemporary scholar's desire to understand the text rather than from the text itself, according to von Rad. Consequently he insisted that Old Testament theology free itself from rigid systems imposed upon the text from without, and set the text free to speak in its own categories and on its own terms. Just how little concerned he was with methodology, which may in itself be described as an unconscious system, has been pointed out by von Rad's first doctoral student and long-time colleague, Rolf Rendtorff.[42] According to Rendtorff, even von Rad's students learned methodology only by doing it, never by means of their teacher's reflection on methodology as such. Rendtorff supports this thesis by calling attention to the imprecise terminology in von Rad's writings, evidence in Rendtorff's view, not of slovenly composition but of an absence of any real concern to perfect a method that would be applicable in every instance.

Rendtorff has conveniently brought together many of the terms von Rad used to describe the complex tradition process.[43] *Tradition* and *Überlieferung* are used synonymously, thus doubling the number of possible terms. Tradition is made up of little tradition matter, tradition components and particles, elements of tradition, tradition moments, tradition material, and tradition substance. The larger complexes are tradition circles, tradition units, tradition blocks, tradition groups, tradition series, tradition clusters, tradition masses, bodies of tradition, and organs of tradition. The mingling of two different traditions results in layers of tradition, while the historical process and changes in the traditions can be understood as tradition process or viewed as lines of tradition and tradition streams. Discontinuity of traditions is called a break in tradition. While one must not expect the literary products from several decades to agree in terminology—or even in substance—and one must grant a scholar the freedom to vary his vocabulary, still there is an element of truth in Friedrich Baumgärtel's accusation that von Rad does not operate with sufficiently precise definitions of crucial categories.[44]

The excessive systematization against which von Rad placed himself so adamantly was essentially a characteristic of German scholarship. Here as in other ways there is a certain provincialism to von Rad's work that is not entirely the result of the war and consequently is in some respects astonishing. Porteous has pointed to the situation in German theology that called forth the fundamental emphases of von Rad's theological approach.[45] The concern to glorify God as the sole source of salvation, that is, the insistence that salvation is the work of God and not man, gave voice to the ringing proclamation of God's mighty acts. Faith, it was believed, followed redemption; Israel's response to God's saving deeds bore witness to the truth of the Protestant doctrine that grace precedes demand, or in another word, law. Again the emphasis on the confessions of Israel's faith in God's saving deeds was an attempt to counteract the nineteenth-century tendency to psychologize, that is, to analyze the religious experience of ancient Israel. It was precisely this skeleton in the closet of

Old Testament scholarship, best seen in Gustav Hölscher's book on the prophets (*Die Profeten*), that prompted von Rad to insist that Old Testament theology be something other than a history of Israel's religion. Von Rad's acknowledged failure in this respect must have been particularly vexing; furthermore the additional charge made by Baumgärtel that the result of von Rad's theology is *chaos for the minister*[46] must have been especially painful to one who felt so keenly the responsibility of assisting ministers in their endeavor to understand God's word preserved in ancient texts.

A remarkable feature of von Rad's theology is the attempt to bring together the two Testaments,[47] a concern that cannot be entirely divorced from the struggle with national socialism and its disdain for everything Jewish. Convinced that the ancient church had shown wisdom in her insistence against Marcion that the Old Testament was inspired scripture, von Rad sought to relate the two Testaments by means of the hermeneutical principle known as typology. But this typological exegesis differed from traditional typology at one decisive point. Essentially, von Rad believed that the Old Testament was full of promise and fulfillment, and that each fulfillment opened up the possibility of additional promise and greater fulfillment. This principle of interpretation suggested that the Old Testament leans toward the New. Consequently, von Rad sought to show how certain types (for instance, the suffering anointed one) corresponded to antitypes; he insisted, however, that the Old Testament categories should not be denigrated at the expense of New Testament concepts. In no case would he admit the correctness of the shadow/substance analogy, for the Old Testament contained, in von Rad's view, both elements. So also did the New Testament.

Not entirely unrelated to this notion of promise and fulfillment is the remarkable fact that von Rad saw in the prophetic movement a decisive break in Israelite confessional statements. Whereas all other traditions are said to be oriented toward the past, the prophets turn to the future in genuine eschatological openness to divine action. The emphasis shifts, according to von Rad, from what God has done to what God is getting ready to do. Perhaps the difference is partly attributable to the cultic setting of the former and the noncultic character of the prophetic movement, for cultic response is by its very nature conservative and celebrative of past saving events which, it is hoped, will be renewed in the present situation of worship. That is, reactualization or representation is the *raison d'être* of the cult. Unresolved, however, is the question: "How does one relate the eschatological prophetic expectation to the Christian claim of a final fulfillment within the New Testament?"

But the peeling off of tradition layer by layer even within the Old Testament itself created a new danger, specifically the playing off of the final stage against the initial one, with which it was often in tension. Von Rad argued that the text must be understood in light of its original intention, but he also maintained with equal conviction that attention should be given to every distinct stage of the tradition too. Gradually he came to emphasize the depth dimension and truth claim of the text as a way out of the false dilemma, that is, the choice between the original or the final sense of the text. Such an overview of the textual tradition led von Rad to a profound appreciation of the literary craftsmanship of those responsible for the final form of the tradition. The result was a penetrating analysis of the great literary complexes in the Old Testament: the Yahwist, Elohist, Deuteronomist, Priestly Writer, Succession document, the story of David's rise to power, and the Chronicler.

Tradition cannot flourish unless it has a locus, a setting in which it is allowed to wield its extraordinary power to renew life. Von Rad was not satisfied with Gunkel's proposed answer to this problem in terms of professional storytellers sitting around the fireside and entertaining their audiences with the etiological sagas in Genesis. Genesis was more than explanations for diverse languages, sexual desire, enmity of serpents, pillars of salt, and destruction of towns. Von Rad followed Sigmund Mowinckel, the foremost Scandinavian literary critic of the time, whose publications opened a wholly new understanding of Psalms, in recognizing the central role of the cult in ancient Israel, and correspondingly a certain fixity of tradition that militated against all but a bare minimum of creativity and originality. Indeed, a fundamental premise of von Rad's writing is the assumption (following Martin Buber, the Jewish philosopher whose categories of I-Thou and I-It have entered everyday speech) that early Israel prior to the Solomonic enlightenment is best characterized by the term *pan sacrality*. By pan sacrality von Rad called attention to the sacred character of every dimension of life. Accordingly, von Rad searched the Scriptures diligently for evidence of ancient cultic festivals; he believed he found proof for festivals associated with seasonal changes (Feast of Weeks, and Tabernacles), as well as others (Covenant Renewal ceremony at Shechem). While in his more cautious moments he admitted the hypothetical nature of such conclusions,[48] this did not prevent von Rad from making full hermeneutical (interpretative) use of his provisional conclusions. Thus every facet of early Israel's life, whether warfare, legal administration, royal ritual, or personal piety, was brought under the umbrella of the cult and provided with its appropriate festival and sanctuary. The vulnerability of this wall in von Rad's monumental bastion was quickly perceived, and critics concentrated their heavy artillery upon this area until von Rad was forced to concede that he had possibly overstated his case.[49]

The radical difference between us moderns and the ancient Israelite lent credence to von Rad's sacral emphasis. A corollary

is the unity of nature and history in Israel, in sharp contrast to
our careful distinction of these categories. In the Old Testament,
creation itself was understood as an event in history. Refusing
to choose between the two ways of interpreting reality, the ancient and the modern, von Rad sought to bring about a dialogue
between modern readers and the biblical text, which cast a question mark over our own understanding at any point in time. But
only if the same reality is spoken of in both the text and by
modern interpreters can there be a real challenge to the contemporary view. Wolfhart Pannenberg, a student of von Rad
whose attempt to prove historicity of the revelatory event in
Jesus Christ, and around whom a theological movement has
formed, has recognized that von Rad's work sought to expose
the poverty of modern thought and to provide an apologia for
the aesthetic, or full person.[50] In this regard von Rad came to
realize that there is genuine faith (trust) in all knowledge. The
failure to recognize mystery or limits to our knowledge, von
Rad argued, is symptomatic of the poverty of modern thought,
even if it arose as a necessary rejection of perverted faith that
in its way also robs life of genuine mystery.

Von Rad's decisive move in the direction of meditation may
be traceable in part to this struggle to relate the ancient world
view to the modern one. As early as 1960 he decried our help-
lessness to read and to proclaim the Bible,[51] and saw in this fact
sure signs that there is something sick in us. The added personal
confession of such sickness shows how keenly von Rad felt the
perversion of relationship with Transcendence. It is noteworthy
that his last three published works show an increasing concern
to wrestle with the problem of divine silence, a point overlooked
by Lothar Perlitt in his stimulating essay, "The Hiddenness of
God." [52]

In this experience of the silence of God, we moderns find our-
selves in the same situation that befell the Deuteronomist, for

whom God had ceased to speak. The central place occupied by this work in von Rad's thought corresponds to his view of its role in the history of Israel's traditions. According to him Deuteronomy represents a significant revival movement in ancient Israel, around 622 B.C.E., a blotting out of centuries of apostasy, and a return to the original decision situation when a people with staff in hand faced the awesome and hopeful prospect of divine leadership as communicated through Moses. Given the signal importance ascribed to this proclamation of the law in the context of grace, it is not surprising that von Rad returned to Deuteronomy for instruction as if consulting a compass while on the high seas. Not once or twice, but three times he endeavored to comprehend the heart of the Book of Deuteronomy, and this activity spanned the greater part of his academic career.[53] While he stoutly resisted any claim to the discovery of a center in the Old Testament, at the same time von Rad permitted Deuteronomy to come very close to functioning in the same way the Christ event did in the literature of the New Testament.

To sum up, I have tried to call attention to the dominant theses in von Rad's illustrious career and have pointed to some fundamental problems as yet unresolved. But in keeping with Porteous's judicious counsel,[54] I do not intend to launch a broadside against one whose achievements would stand long after any puny attack had managed to open a breach here and there. Even the perspective from which I write is largely shaped by von Rad, although I part company with him at many crucial junctures. What I envision, therefore, is a dialogue with the texts which von Rad has provided, as an aid to the understanding of the depth dimension in the biblical text.

This dialogue will attempt to grasp von Rad's thought from four perspectives. The first takes its departure from his fundamental premise that the Old Testament consists of ancient confessional traditions. Our task will be, therefore, to come to

grips with these traditions as he saw them, chief of which will
be those of holy war, the ark and the tent, the exodus (and
accompanying traditions of wilderness, conquest, patriarchs,
and primeval history), the Sinai, and the Davidic-Zion tradition
complexes. But these traditions were dependent upon human
transmitters, both for their preservation and for the alterations
that kept them viable from generation to generation. A chapter
will therefore be devoted to the examination of the most important transmitters: the Yahwist, Elohist, Deuteronomist, Priestly
Writer, Chronicler, prophets, and sages.

According to von Rad, the primary means by which these
transmitters communicated their special traditions was through
the creation of "historical portraits," [55] that is, the fleshing out
of their perspectives in human characters whose lives demonstrate both the noble and the tragic responses to God's direction
of their lives. Such ciphers or portraits rest behind depictions
of Moses, Abraham, Joseph, David, and Jeremiah (of the *via
dolorosa*). Hence we shall take a close look at these figures as
von Rad envisioned them, discovering therefrom the aspirations
and anxieties of ancient Israel.

We cannot simply lift these characters out of their cultural
setting, so alien to us, and set them down in the twentieth century, where they would be completely out of place. This means
that a chapter must be devoted to a clarification of the world
view of ancient Israel, particularly the difficult question of the
relationship between nature and history. This section will discuss the enrichment of redemption theology through creation,
to use von Rad's phrase. But it will also attempt to reintroduce
the element of law or demand into theological discussion by
relating the doctrine of creation to the idea of divine justice, a
natural next step to von Rad's analysis of the doxology of judgment.[56] To do so we shall focus upon von Rad's special interest
during his final years, namely the problem of divine silence

and the accompanying doubt or despair on the one hand and absolute trust on the other. This section will, of course, concentrate on von Rad's interpretation of wisdom literature. These four approaches, then, should provide different avenues to the thought of one whose total contribution to the understanding of the Old Testament and whose influence upon his peers is second to none.

II. The Traditions

HOLY WAR

In von Rad's little book, *Holy War in Ancient Israel*,[1] we encounter von Rad's methodology at its zenith. In many ways the study of the sacral institution of holy war provides the best access to the author's manner of interpreting biblical texts. Inasmuch as the ideology of holy war pervades the literature of the Old Testament, with some notable exceptions, we shall initiate our discussions of von Rad's understanding of the chief historical traditions of Israel at precisely this point.

The book begins with a word about the nature of the texts in which holy war receives conscious or unconscious attestation. Between the actual period of the institution of holy war, that is, the time of the judges, (c. 1100 B.C.E.) and the literary composition of these narratives (6th c.) stand centuries of Israelite history. In this interval much had transpired that altered the understanding of warfare, on the one hand, and divine activity, on the other. In short, the Solomonic "Enlightenment"[2] stands

like a towering mountain obscuring the vision of the valley beyond. Of necessity, then, the narrators wrote about holy war of
bygone days in terms of their own understanding of warfare,
since they had neither the inclination nor the wherewithal to
scale the mountain peaks that obstructed their vision of the real
character of that about which they wrote. The result is a strange
mixture of ancient traditions and "current" ideology; holy war
is thus viewed through the eyes of one who has had no experience with the institution as a living reality.

To separate the ancient historical core from the subsequent
accretions of time and artistic design is the task to which von
Rad addresses himself. What is attempted is nothing less than
tracing the entire history of an institution on the basis of texts
whose date is at best conjectural. How is this difficult goal to be
achieved? Von Rad opts for the constructing of a "model" of
holy war from select texts of probable early date as the first
stage, to be followed by testing the accuracy of the hypothetical
construct on the basis of the biblical texts. Precisely how this
method is supposed to solve the above problem, however, is
difficult to perceive. Actually a prior understanding of holy war
determines the choice of texts that supposedly preserve a heavy
precipitate of earlier traditions, and the operative criteria are
by no means self-evident. We shall see how arbitrary decisions
will have to be made time and again when the texts themselves
offer no conclusive evidence as to which side of the Solomonic
"Enlightenment" is determinative for them.

What, in von Rad's eyes, was this decisive moment in Israel's
intellectual history that imposes itself between the earlier pan
sacrality and a subsequent rationalization or theologization of
outmoded traditions and institutions? It was nothing less than
a complete emancipation from patriarchal ties, a cutting of the
umbilical cord in matters sacral. Prior to this time all of life
was centered in the cult; [3] here resided the means of life and

death, and in the sanctuary every member of the tribal amphictyony found his *raison d'être*. Now suddenly a new spirit
surges through the internationalized court of Solomon, in part
due to foreign influence but also in large measure attributable
to a certain readiness on Israel's part to have done with the
sacral institutions that arose in an entirely different situation
and have lost their power to sustain faith in this alien environment. This new spirit of humanism created its own media of
communication: great narrative complexes and didactic wisdom.
Proper rhetoric, an interest in natural phenomena, the cultiva-
tion of the individual by means of ideal portraits (*Bildungs-
ideal*), an inclination toward sensitivity, psychologization and
subjectivity—such was the scope of the fresh spirit that swept
through Solomon's court which basked in the splendor of newly
acquired wealth, general well-being, and peace on all sides.[4]

Now it is to be observed that this picture of Solomonic "Enlightenment" rests upon a dating of biblical texts that is far
from certain. Remove one or two key narrative complexes from
this setting and the entire edifice crumbles.[5] Once again a decision has been made as to the probable provenance of novelistic
material; proof for this choice is not deemed necessary, in the
same way that it is said to be self-evident that holy war was
sacral. Now that may be true if one accepts the validity of
Martin Buber's claim that early Israelite religion is best characterized by the term pan sacrality. However, it is by no means an
established fact that such a cultic umbrella stood over ancient
Israel's daily life. It would necessarily follow that if von Rad
were mistaken about this phenomenon he would be equally at
fault in viewing the Solomonic period as the emancipation from
bondage to pan sacrality, which never in fact existed.

Our confidence in the methodology becomes a little weaker
when we see a model of holy war constructed from unrelated
texts spanning several centuries, an ideal model that admittedly

was never realized fully in history. What we are presented with in these pages is an idealized picture (*Urbild*), a datum of faith! Von Rad does not seem to be bothered unduly by this tension between real and fabricated, to make the distinction in extreme language, for the latter has a reality of its own that possesses the power to shape the course of history.[6]

On the other hand, he *is* troubled by the conflict between the actual course of historical events surrounding the entrance into Palestine by the early tribes of Israel and the idealized description of these events. Relying heavily upon the negative findings in this area by his mentor Alt, von Rad rejects the principle delineations of the conquest stories as a distortion of what actually transpired when the small band of Leah tribes entered the Land of Promise. In this instance, let it be noted, von Rad rejects the "ideal portrait" in favor of the less grandiose account of the situation given by the modern critical historian. Justification for such inconsistency he would probably find in the fact that holy war was an institution—sacral, that is—and that the credibility gap was significantly less in the case of holy war. After all, holy war was a reality that none could deny;[7] the same could not be said for the violent conquest of Canaan by the twelve tribes of Israel.

What shape did holy war assume in von Rad's view? Two ideas stand out above all else: holy war was purely defensive, and it was voluntary. The other components arise from these two facts. Imperiled by attack from without, the people of God enlist the aid of their fellows by means of gruesome testimony to the injustice perpetrated and danger hovering over them (Judg. 19:29; 1 Sam. 11:7), or they sound the horn that announces a military engagement. A ringing response was by no means assured, for the desire to do what was right in one's own eyes—the poignant theme of the scandalous stories in Judges 17–21 [8]—was stronger than ties of kinship and religion. Hence

Deborah singles out the willingness of certain tribes to come to
the assistance of those threatened, as if she were somewhat sur-
prised that covenanted groups could put the common welfare
above personal safety. Those who came are called the people
of God; they are under sacral orders, hence avoid sex, make
vows, and maintain laws of ritual purity since God is in their
midst. He must be consulted about whether to go to war or not;
if the oracle is negative, a ceremony of repentance is held, but
if positive, the leader cries, "Yahweh has given . . . into your
hands." On this divine oracle rests the full confidence of victory
that characterizes holy war. Yahweh goes before his army and
fights his war to defend his people, whose proper attitude is
complete faith. The person who fails in this one essential is to
be sent home. Now comes the moment of divine terror, the complete panic that envelopes the enemy camp as the victorious
shout of God's people reaches their ears. Yahweh wins the battle
alone, although other texts speak synergistically of divine-
human cooperation (Yahweh comes to assist his army). The
spoil is holy, under the ban (ḥerem); all living creatures are to
be put to death, and precious metals are from this moment holy
to the Lord. The dispersion of the victorious people follows the
cry, "To your tents, O Israel." To this setting is said to belong
the origin of two fundamental theological concepts: faith and
the people of God.

There is some question as to the precise meaning of the ban;
von Rad thinks the idea of it as a vow is later than the notion
of demand, since the former permits choice. It is strange that he
failed to perceive the tension between absolute demand in the
case of the ban and fully voluntary participation in the case of
the people upon whom this ban becomes obligatory, although it
could be argued that those who come of their own volition become subject to the conditions of holy war. In any event, the
ban became a *status confessionis* at some stage in Israel's his-

tory, as the conflict between Samuel and Saul over the disposition of spoil shows clearly (1 Sam. 15).

So much for the datum of faith. Now how does it fare in the
course of history? This question occupies the center of von
Rad's attention for the greater part of *Holy War in Ancient
Israel*, for it is the history of a theological tradition that com-
mands his complete interest. Four literary stages in the tradition
are singled out: ancient Israel, post-Solomonic "historical"
accounts, prophecy and Deuteronomy. Von Rad thinks he can
discern evidence of a certain rationalization and theologization
of holy war, a shifting of emphasis to miracle and concomitant
faith, and a subjectivization and individualization of piety. In
short, he thinks the sacral institution was severed from its cultic
moorings and allowed to float in alien waters until its eventual
return to the cult in the form of the piety of the worshiper whose
voice is echoed in the Psalms.

The first stage of holy war, that of ancient Israel prior to the
monarchy, is shrouded in darkness due to the literary fiction of
a single onslaught upon Canaan by all Israel. Von Rad refuses
to attribute the total picture to fancy, however, and grants the
validity of Martin Noth's conjectural amphictyonic bond ce-
menting the Leah tribes from the very earliest times.[9] Nevertheless, von Rad thinks our knowledge of cultic matters from this
period is negligible, and limits his observations about holy war
to the time of the judges. Even these narratives, he concedes, are
told from the later standpoint and hence are not fully sacral.
Where we have duplicate accounts, the one poetry and the other
prose, as in the Deborah episode, there is a recognizable tension
between the sacred and the profane (Judg. 4–5).

Von Rad interprets each of the narratives from this period in
the light of the above model, judging those elements that accord
with it to be indicative of holy war and relegating those at
variance with the hypothetical construct to later rationalization.

Accordingly, emphasis is laid on charismatic leadership, defensive warfare, summons and voluntary response, divine victory, the ban, the oracle and the like. Holy war centers upon such heroes as Saul, Gideon, Ehud, Deborah, and Jephthah, although the latter is said to represent the tension between the literary view of battle and holy war. Analysis of these narratives prompts von Rad to ask the not altogether rhetorical question: "Was all war at this time holy?" The grandiose visions of power behind Abimelech's behavior and the Danite struggle for living space suggest for him a negative answer to this query. Still there are many unsolved questions from this fund of traditions, not the least of which has to do with terminology. Von Rad notes that the leader was certainly not called *judge*; but he shuns the making of a decision between the options of *qatsin* or *moshia*[10]. At all events he is convinced that the magical world stands on the other side of holy war, and concludes on the basis of an absence of myth in holy war that the institution antedates the Canaanization of Israel's faith.

A decisive change in holy war came with the Israelite monarchy. Saul and David waged offensive war with mercenary soldiers; von Rad sees in this development the demise of holy war as a sacral institution. Actually, von Rad admits, the new departure had been holy war's practice of using ordinary citizens for warfare, for the history of mercenary soldiers reaches far back in human interrelationships. With Solomon, horses and chariots were pressed into service to guard the monarch's great wealth; this necessitated a special kind of professional soldier and fortified cities. Even among the professionals, remnants of holy war ideology survive, von Rad maintains. Proof of such a claim he finds in Uriah's refusal to enjoy the pleasures of sex while his comrades were at war and in Joab's recognition that the Lord does as he pleases, both of which are readily explained from other presuppositions. Uriah may have been justifiably suspicious of David's motives for bringing him home to a (pregnant) wife, and the idea that man proposes but God disposes, that is, the ever present contingency in human affairs, is by no means limited to holy war.[11]

In the literature written during this heyday of Solomonic Enlightenment, when the narrator finally achieves sovereign freedom over his materials and develops stylistic media from tragedy to burlesque, four essential types of holy war are discernible. In the first, the sacking of Jericho is accomplished neither by force of arms nor through divine battle, but by magic alone. Another type is represented in the battle between Gideon and the Midianites; here the miracle is emphasized and the paltry army of Gideon does not lift a sword. Furthermore, rational explanations are provided and the story probes the inner thoughts, fears and dreams of the enemy. Von Rad labels the spirit of this narrative "secular and uncultic, almost Protestant." A third kind of account can be found in Exodus 14, where the miraculous stands out impressively, but where the inner attitude of the people and the rhetoric of Moses are highlighted. Here faith follows the wondrous event, and its object is an astonishing combination ("So they believed the Lord and his servant Moses"). Here, too, the inner thoughts of the enemy are stressed. The fourth type is represented by the conflict between David and Goliath. Direct speeches fill the account to the bursting point; eighteen appear, laying stress upon the youthful David's unpreparedness for battle, his dauntless courage, his dependence upon Yahweh, and the like. Here holy war has almost become the occasion of a sermon; the decisive word is David's confession, which *evokes* faith. In this instance holy war and the use of weapons are mutually contradictory, and the miracle is emphasized. Indeed, the story comes to a close with a reference to the *friendship* of David and Jonathan! Von Rad does not view these four types as sequential; rather they breathe the didactic and kerygmatic spirit of the Solomonic and post-Solomonic humanism.

Now it might be expected that the prophets of Israel would insist upon a return to the earlier ideology of holy war, inasmuch as charisma [12] played a greater role in their thought than royal birth. But, von Rad observes, holy war is not a decisive key to the interpretation of Isaiah, the one prophet who made the most extensive use of holy war traditions. Tension did surface quite early, however, between kingship and holy war ideology. Testimony to this bitter conflict is given in the story of Saul and the Amelakites; here nine verses record the battle, while the rest of the long chapter narrates subsequent events (1 Sam. 15). Von Rad writes that this story has no historical value for the relationships between Saul and Samuel, although it does preserve a reminiscence of tension between the State and sacral traditions, while the original point of the story, the ban, is nearly lost. It is noteworthy that prophecy is here seen as the preserver of patriarchal holy war traditions. Von Rad finds confirmation of such a prophetic function in ninth-century charismatic leaders associated with Israel's kings who wage war (1 Kings 20), despite the fact that kings rather than charismatic figures lead the troops. Elisha's appellative, "My father, the chariots of Israel and their steeds," is understood as strongly polemical: only the prophet guaranteed divine assistance. Von Rad describes this title as an elementary word of self-consciousness. A decisive step was taken by Isaiah, who internalized and spiritualized holy war's demand for faith (7:1–9) and insisted that strength lay in trust rather than in horses and alliances (30:15). The impact of Exodus 14 upon Isaiah is determinative; there is here no place for human action. Instead, Isaiah insists that Israel look to the Lord (22:8–11), and opposes arms and coalitions (31:1–4); here the contrast between flesh and spirit is that between a lack of charisma and the presence of charisma. For him the prophet alone is the charismatic leader; kings Ahaz and Hezekiah have no claim to this gift. Von Rad also discerns the presence of holy war ideology in Amos 2:14–16 (divine terror), Micah 4:11–13 (an eschatological holy war), Ezekiel 38:19–22 (divine confusion and panic, earthquake, hail), Haggai 2:21–22, and Zechariah 4:6. It is not clear to von Rad why holy war remains on the periphery of prophetic thought except in Isaiah, where it is the burning message next to the David/Zion traditions. But even Isaiah never renewed the *cultic sphere* of holy war; for prophecy, holy war remained tradition rather than sacral institution.

How does it happen that holy war, which has ceased as an institution in Israel, is brought to life again in the great revival movement, Deuteronomy? Von Rad postulates the following explanation. In 701 B.C.E. the professional army of Judah was completely annihilated. Yet within a short period an entire military contingent was mustered by Josiah. How was this possible? Holy war ideology had been preserved by the people of the land, the landed peasantry. These people of God saw their golden opportunity with Josiah and gave him wholehearted support. Deuteronomy, with genuine holy war traditions alongside rationalizing humane tendencies that viewed holy war as an offensive battle against the Canaanite cult, provided the great literary fiction for their voluntary army. Its message proclaimed that the Lord who dwells in heaven was also present in battle; Levitical speeches with didactic import actualize old traditions for God's people who march forth to purify the land of an alien cult. The result was catastrophic; here was the ultimate demise of holy war.

Any subsequent use of holy war ideology is thoroughly spiritualized, whether in 2 Chronicles (20:1–30), the final stage of development toward spiritual sublimation, or Psalms 24:8; 147:10–11; 33:16–19. Here is an ideal piety for the *individual* (cf. Jer. 17:5–8), and holy war has returned to the cult; but an army, horses, and so forth are no longer a real possibility. Such is the history of a sacral institution which gave birth to and nurtured the important spiritual concepts of *faith* and the *people* of God.

THE TENT AND THE ARK

Joshua 3:11 brings the ark into intimate connection with holy war.[13] Here Yahweh's going forth to battle in front of the people is replaced by the ark. At times it even seems as if the ark and Yahweh are one and the same. Elsewhere the stories about the fate of the ark not only give the impression that all Israel, instead of a local voluntary contingent, goes to war (the army is called the children of *Israel*), but they also dispense with the charismatic leader. Inasmuch as the ark likewise belonged to ancient Israel's sacral life, a look at its tradition history will throw additional light on the institutions of ancient Israel. But we cannot advance very far along this route before coming upon another cultic tradition, that of the tent, which has been interwoven with the traditions of the ark. Often the resulting tradition threatens to burst forth in opposite directions, so alien are the ideologies of tent and ark. Despite this tension, "There is no other institution which remained for so long at the very heart of theological thinking as did the tent and the ark." [14]

A study of these two traditions is informative for yet another reason. The preceding treatment of holy war has restricted itself to the historical tradition of a single sacral institution. But few traditions in ancient Israel occupied such a solitary position; on the contrary, traditions usually came into contact with related and opposing ones at an early stage in their development and vied for place of prominence and even for survival. In such a struggle the tradition that proved to be flexible, adapting to changing situations, had a better chance of surviving than the one that refused to bend with the times. Of necessity, then, variations in the traditions occur, and sometimes mutations. The history of the interrelationship of tent and ark illustrates this point well.

Now traditions become the rallying points of quite distinct theological parties.[15] It can even be said that the strengths or weaknesses of a tradition are dependent upon the fate of those for whom it is regulative. Precisely what role do tent and ark play in the theology of Israel? In a word, the tent tradition is that of a meeting place between men and God who dwells in heaven, while the ark symbolizes a divine enthronement, a dwelling on earth. It can readily be seen that the two concepts are mutually exclusive, von Rad argues, since *presence* and *meeting* contradict one another. Nevertheless the Solomonic temple brings together both traditions and strains them to the breaking point; the tension between these alien concepts is never resolved, although the New Testament opts for the validity of the tent tradition as a more accurate portrayal of God's dealings with man in Jesus of Nazareth.

How does one disentangle the tent and ark traditions that flowed together for centuries like two currents in a single stream? Von Rad does not choose to begin with a model and test it by examining the texts, as is the case in the study of holy war. Rather at this stage of his thought (exactly twenty years earlier than the discussion of holy war) he begins at the final stage of tradition and works backward. His attention is limited to the cultic history of tent and ark; entirely outside his interest span stand the historical (political) issues related to both, as well as the concern of the archeologist to discover cultural artifacts.

Since the Chronicler represents the final development in historical traditions, von Rad begins here. Chronicles is no alien ground to him, for he had already published a careful study of

the "historical imagery" of the work of the Chronicler.[16] Von
Rad calls special attention to the manner in which the latter
counters the tabernacle (tent) theology of the Priestly Writer;
in short, Chronicles takes up the ancient tradition of the ark,
which he associates with the Levites, to combat the Aaronite
tabernacle tradition. The Priestly Writer, too, had found room
for the ark, but in distorted form. For him it is a chest or con-
tainer into which were placed the holy tablets of the law. This
chest, which rests inside the tent, has a special cover of utmost
significance, for it is here that God speaks with Moses. The
Lord's dwelling place is heaven; it is even said that he presents
himself (*ya'ad* in the Niphal, the form usually rendered passive or reflexive; *ya'ad* means that God must be thought to reside
elsewhere—in von Rad's view). But he also dwells in the tent,
von Rad argues, since the ceremonies associated with the offerings take place *before Yahweh*. This notion of divine presence
connected with the ark has not been assimilated by the Priestly
Writer to the contrary idea of the tent as a meeting place of
God and man. Nor have the ideas of a cloud (*'anan*), which
periodically hovers over the tent and symbolizes God's presence
and the *kabod* (glory) of Yahweh which fills the dwelling been
reconciled with the opposing traditions (Exod. 33). Furthermore, von Rad contends, the idea of the cherubim as human in
form, which grows out of the Priestly Writer's refusal to view
the ark solely as a throne, cannot be an accurate element of the
tradition.

If both the Chronicler and the Priestly Writer are guilty of
special retouching of the traditions under discussion, what about
the book in which northern traditions are preserved? Inasmuch
as the heavens themselves cannot contain God, there can be no
talk about the ark as a throne of the deity. Therefore Deuteronomy views the ark as a receptacle for the tablets of the law,
and even coins the phrase "Ark of the Covenant." This idea,

writes von Rad, is entirely new; the ark now becomes what it has never been in reality, namely a receptacle for the tablets of the law. And yet the name *'aron* clearly suggests a box as the oldest meaning of the object under discussion! It is far from clear how such a judgment accords with the purported methodology, for one has the suspicion that a "model" is operating at least unconsciously. Von Rad goes further to deny to Deuteronomy any tent tradition, inasmuch as Deuteronomy 31:14–15 is universally attributed to the Elohist, who knows only the tabernacle tradition. What, then, of the Deuteronomistic school? The crucial text is 1 Kings 8, Solomon's dedicatory prayer. In this Solomonic legend it is plainly said that Yahweh will dwell in the darkness of the temple (8:12–13). Von Rad claims that this text testifies to a flowing together of both traditions, tent and ark. But the removal of the cherubim from the ark weakens the concept of the ark as a divine throne in favor of the Egyptian rationalizing view of cherubim as protectors. Furthermore other traditions intrude at one decisive point (8:11, 12, 27), where reference is made to divine indwelling, the cloud, and heaven as God's place of residence.

Nevertheless, the Deuteronomistic history preserves the authentic understanding of the ark as a throne for the deity. Twice the stories of the ark refer to Yahweh who sits enthroned upon the cherubim (1 Sam. 4:4; 2 Sam. 6:2). Moreover, when the Lord appears to the lad Samuel who is sleeping before the ark, Yahweh is said to *stand forth* (1 Sam. 3:10). He does not have to come, for he dwells on his throne, the ark. The same idea occurs in 2 Kings 19:15, where King Hezekiah spreads Sennacherib's arrogant letter out before the Lord and appeals for help to Yahweh who is "enthroned above the cherubim." Additional proof for such a view is found in Jeremiah 3:16–17, where an equation is made between ark and throne (cf. Ezek. 43:7). Von Rad chooses this interpretation as inherently more

probable, and moves on to an attempt to verify such a decision
from the findings of archeology. On the basis of Assyrian
winged creatures that bear Ishtar's image and Phoenecian
cherubim which function as a divine throne, von Rad thinks that
the idea of the ark as a throne for the deity is irrefutable. But
he refuses to follow Hugo Gressmann in seeing the ark as an
actual throne upon which were placed images of bulls.[17] It is
unfortunate that von Rad did not take into consideration the
implications of Jeroboam's attempt to compete with David's
ancient cultic object, the ark, by returning to an equally old
cultic object, the bull. Such a probable interpretation of Jeroboam's action lends credibility to Gressmann's theory, already
supported somewhat by the old story of the Golden Calf (Exod.
32).[18] The idea of a throne for the deity, of divine dwelling or
presence, implies permanence. How, von Rad asks, could such
a notion have developed in the desert, where a people were forever on the move? Could it be that the early narratives that
introduce the ark into the Moses and Sinai traditions are
anachronistic? Such a conclusion is demanded, he thinks, by
the nature of the stories, for they present *logically impossible
situations*. For example, Numbers 10:33–36, and 14:44 describe an encampment with the tent outside while the ark rests
within the camp itself. The anachronistic character of these
texts does not prevent von Rad from using Numbers 10:35–36
to confirm the suspicion that the ark was a throne; here Yahweh
is instructed to "rise up" and to "be seated." But if the ark does
not derive from the desert tradition, does it even belong to
Yahwism?

The Phoenician idea of Astarte's empty throne borne by
cherubim prompts von Rad to cast a glance in the direction of
Canaan as the possible provenance of the ark. Once this possibility is entertained, supporting evidence rushes to his aid. Von
Rad admits that the title "ark of God" occurs six times less than

the similar "ark of Yahweh." But, he notes, the latter is used by design! Most of the occurences of *'aron Yahweh* come in the stories dealing with the fate of the ark in Philistine territory. It was precisely in such contests that a point had to be made of the God involved. Thus the emphasis upon Yahweh is natural. This means, von Rad concludes, that the original title associated with the ark tradition was "ark of God" (*'aron ha'elohim*), and therefore, the ark is of Canaanite origin. Lest this adoption of an alien sacral institution be understood as apostasy or a great loss to Israelite faith, von Rad points to three areas in which enrichment resulted.

The first area in which the theology of the ark deepened Israelite faith derives from the concept of enthronement. If Yahweh is understood as dwelling among his people, it follows that they can be confident of his continued presence. Hence Israel can march to battle with complete assurance that her God is with her. This confidence does not come, von Rad argues, at the expense of the conviction that Yahweh is also the Lord of creation. The second area of enrichment is closely related; the ark becomes the symbol of divine protection. This focal point for the idea of Yahweh as the nation's protector has its special title for God: "Yahweh of hosts." [19] In short, "national religion and the ark are inseparable." [20] But the ideas associated with the ark also introduced a buoyant optimism into Israel's worship, tempering the severity of justice with a generous measure of mercy, according to von Rad. It must be remembered that it was before the ark that David danced with joy, that "the Deuteronomist, who stands in the full stream of the tradition of the ark, never tires of promoting cultic rejoicing (*simhah*)," [21] and at the end of the line stands the Chronicler whose worship consists almost entirely of praise.

Should further defense of the Canaanite origin of the ark be deemed necessary, one can appeal to several things. Canaanite, not Israelite, are the cultic building, the sacred lamp (*ner*), the oracle of incubation,[22] the cultic dance, and the connection with the autumn festival. While von Rad may be right in seeing each of these as non-Israelite *in origin,* the evidence is far from conclusive. It should be noted that Samuel was not *seeking* an oracle; the story certainly intends to highlight the unexpected nature of the call, which must be repeated three times. Hence we have no right to speak of incubation. Furthermore, it is hazardous to argue on the basis of what happens to the tradition during Solomon's time—specifically the association of the ark with a temple—that this new departure, for Israel at least, was original to the ark.

Von Rad recognizes the polemical nature of Nathan's speech to David, which rejects the idea of the ark as embodied in the very concept of a temple (2 Sam. 7:5-7). The attack against the ark is based on the tabernacle tradition, the conviction that Yahweh dwells in the highest heaven and periodically comes down to meet with chosen representatives of the people. This means, von Rad writes, that Julius Wellhausen's thesis that the tabernacle in the Priestly Writing is the Solomonic temple projected back into the period of the wilderness sojourn is patently false.[23] The temple expresses divine dwelling, while the tent points to a coming from above, to God's meeting with man.

What, then, has our journey into the remote antiquity of Israelite traditions taught us? Just this: that the ancient Israelite idea of a God who comes to meet with his own (tent) has had to vie with a Canaanite concept of divine enthronement (ark), and in the process changes took place as necessary. But neither the tent nor the ark was able to oust the other, and thus tension continued to the end, although "the idea of the tent drove out completely the notion of the ark as a throne, but has absorbed certain essential elements of this conception." [24]

We have suggested above that von Rad is not entirely free

from a tendency to read the biblical texts in the light of an unconscious "model," or preunderstanding. But we must go on to point out another fundamental principle that shapes his conclusions; that principle is logical coherence. Now it is a highly dubious procedure to judge ancient texts so stringently on the basis of coherence, as von Rad himself has often reminded us. In any case, one cannot conceal the suspicion that von Rad has pressed the language of the stories too much at times. This is particularly true of the conclusions drawn from the statement that Yahweh *stood forth* to speak to Samuel, which just as conceivably may apply to the basic issue, enthronement or meeting. Is it absolutely certain that ancient Israel would have understood these notions as mutually exclusive? Would they not be explained more naturally as Israel's response to the mystery of faith? Yahweh was experienced in both manners. He dwelt in their midst, for his presence was a reality; but he was also experienced as absent, so that a coming from afar was likewise appropriate language.

One further observation may be ventured at this point. In the course of an attempt to discover the reason for the tenacity of the term '*aron* (box) for what was understood as a throne, von Rad makes a judgment that will ring forth from the pages of his books for decades to come. That simple claim runs as follows: "On the other hand, Yahweh is the God of history, passionately furthering his own purposes and jealously guarding his unique position." [25]

THE SINAI TRADITION

We have seen how von Rad proceeds to analyze a given theological tradition in ancient Israel. In what follows, I shall attempt to provide a description of the leading traditions in Israel as he saw them. We shall begin with the Sinai tradition, inasmuch as its absence from the credo occasioned considerable discussion in von Rad's analysis of the Hexateuch.

Precisely what did von Rad mean by the Sinai tradition? Composed of two parts, the Yahwistic-Elohistic strand (Exod. 19–24, 32–34) and the Priestly version (Exod. 25–31, 35 to Num. 10:10), this cycle has been secondarily inserted into a block of material which treats events at Kadesh (Exod. 17–18, Num. 10:11–14:45). The predominant elements of the Sinai narrative are the account of a theophany and the making of a covenant.

As in the case of the historical credo, here too von Rad distinguished an original Sinai cycle from later free, poetic variants of the tradition (Deut. 33:2, 4; Judg. 5; Hab. 3). The final stage consisted of cultic legends, although both witnesses to this phenomenon (Pss. 50, 81) indicate that the material has become independent of the cult. Von Rad describes these two texts as secondary poetic compositions that retain cultic characteristics.

The Sinai cycle concentrates on the receipt of the law. Israel arrives at Sinai, Moses ascends the mountain, the people prepare themselves to encounter God, and Moses descends in order to make cultic cleansing a reality. God's self-manifestation takes place on the third day,[26] accompanied by extraordinary signs of divine presence (fire, smoke, trumpet blast). Moses climbs the mountain once again, and receives the Decalogue.[27] There follows the proclamation of that law, the setting up of the tent of meeting, Aaron's sacrifice, God's appearance in all his glory, the people's oath, and a covenantal sacrifice.

The priestly source reports that Moses received instructions for the Tabernacle, and emphasizes the investiture and installation of Aaron and his sons as priests. What the older account had understood as God's revelation for everyday life, the priestly narrator interprets as sacral orders.

The Ten Commandments formed the midpoint of a solemn occasion; at Shechem, this statement of what displeases the Lord was recited every seven years. Intended for laity, the Decalogue shows no interest in priestly concerns. Von Rad notes that the minimal statement lacks positive filling out, but nevertheless points to God who watches over men and women in their humanity.

The Sinai cycle was attached to a place, Sinai, and to a person, Moses. Into this tradition, certain additions have been inserted. Four stand out notably: the golden calf, the aetiology of the Tent, the *Panim* (Face), and the Name of God. The tradition thereby places Aaron and the people in a bad light, and emphasizes God's distance from sinful humanity. Overall, the Sinai cycle moves on three levels: the ordinary plane of everyday affairs, the special legal ordinance required of priests, and the sphere of worship.

In von Rad's view, certain features are lacking in the Sinai tradition. We do not find cosmological elements, the mythic battle against chaos,[28] allusions to the creation of the world, reference to the Lord's enthronement, mention of subjugated nations, and the like. It is apparent, therefore, that prophetic texts which bring together the Sinai tradition and the Davidic tradition failed to make a mark on the priestly account.

Von Rad maintains that when Israel finally incorporated creation traditions into her sacred story, they were relegated to a secondary, supportive role. The only exceptions occur in non-Israelite psalms that have been taken over by Israel (19, 104) and in a narrative (Gen. 14:19) that employs a Canaanite epithet, "Creator of heaven and earth." In genuine Yahwism, creation never attained the stature of a relevant, independent doctrine, von Rad observes. Only in wisdom literature does creation appear as an independent doctrine; there reward and punishment are grounded in a belief in creation rather than the righteousness of the covenant God. Into this reflective category Psalm 8 falls; it speaks about a God who fences man around with providential care.

In demonstrating the accuracy of this claim that creation played a subordinate role in Yahwism, von Rad concentrates upon Deutero-Isaiah, where the soteriological function of creation is clearly discernible.[29] Allusions to God's creative power, always standing in subordinate clauses or in apposition, function to confirm his ability to save. Indeed, creation is ancillary to redemption, and provides a foundation for that message. It thus stimulates confidence in the Lord who saves.

Although belief in creation belongs to the very beginnings of Israelite religious thought, danger from the Canaanite front hindered a full appropriation of this important concept. The decisive breakthrough came when Deutero-Isaiah seized the Canaanite myth of a struggle against chaos and identified it with Yahweh's victory at the Reed sea. In the struggle with the chaos dragon, creation and redemption almost coincide as one saving act. This redemptive understanding of creation enabled Israelite thinkers to make full use of creation motifs without capitulating to an alien religion.

Von Rad insists that the soteriological understanding of creation is the most primitive expression of Yahwistic belief concerning creation. It finds expression in some very old psalms (Pss. 89, 74). To be sure, other psalms contain passages celebrating God's creative and redemptive power as distinct and unrelated (Pss. 136, 148, 33). The doxologies of Amos (4:13; 5:8–9; 9:5–6)[30] move a step beyond this toward the position endorsed by Deutero-Isaiah, in von Rad's thinking.

In the struggle against Baalism,[31] it would have been easy for Israel to argue that nature belongs to Yahweh. According to von Rad, neither Deuteronomy nor Hosea adopted this means of dealing with the problem. Israel's first task was to safeguard redemption. Once that was accomplished, she could take the next step toward broadening and enriching that fundamental understanding of Yahweh.

What view of creation lies behind the priestly and Yahwistic accounts in Genesis 1–2? Von Rad suggests that creation does not occur here for its own sake. On the contrary, it belongs to a history leading to the call of Abraham and culminating in the occupation of the land by God's chosen people. He writes: "Presumptuous as it may sound, creation is part of the aetiology of Israel." [32] From this fact flows a far-reaching theological consequence: creation is understood as a work in time. Therefore, it is perfectly natural that the priestly author marked creation off into days, and that Israel's genealogy began with that event.

Essentially two kinds of statements about creation occur here, the hymnic and the didactic. The former *have* assent, while the latter seek to gain it. Von Rad thinks the Yahwist is considerably more didactic; though older than the priestly account, this Yahwistic text does not provide the key to interpretation.

If creation thinking arose early in Israel, why are texts dealing with the topic comparatively late? Von Rad's answer could be anticipated: revelation had opened up history, not nature. Above all, Yahweh was remembered as the one who delivered an oppressed people from Egyptian bondage.

THE EXODUS TRADITION

Just how did Israel fall into slavery? The primeval history and partriarchal narratives describe humanity's bondage to a greater power, sin. The Yahwist's "great hamartiology," [33] or reflection about sin and its consequences, in Genesis 3–11 describes a road taken that leads step by step into catastrophe. Once sin burst upon the human scene, it fell like an avalanche, sweeping everything into its destructive path. The flood was Yahweh's attempt to blot out this awesome power.

We must view the primeval history from three entirely different perspectives: theological, anthropological, and cultural. Theologically, the story is "fraught with background" (Auerbach), that is, it stimulates the theological imagination through restraint, through what is left unspoken rather than by means of explicit suggestion. Wishing to be like God, men and women abandoned the simplicity of obedience. Hoping to acquire knowledge of all things, they refused to accept a dependent status. Such rebellion led to removal of the boundary between heaven and earth: cohabitation between angels and humans (Gen. 6). While the Yahwist concentrates attention upon sin's incursion and its impact upon people, the priestly writer focuses upon God's action and promulgation of his will for humanity. For both authors, God matched human sin with divine grace.

Seen from an anthropological perspective, the Yahwistic narrative describes sin as a human phenomenon. The story of the fall, for example, shows astonishing insight into the psychology of seduction and guilt. The shame that accompanied this initial rebellion "is the first preconscious sign of a mysterious breach that now permeates his whole physical nature, upon which fear follows as the Fall's second uncanny mark." [34] This rupture in the human situation now spreads to the larger environment, affecting the relationship between man and creatures as well as that between man and God. The multiplication of languages (Gen. 11:1–9) naturally follows such discord among humans, but this story also illustrates human pride, a storming of heaven's gates.

Von Rad puts considerable emphasis upon the cultural perspective of the primeval history. The fundamental relationship between humans and the soil breaks down, and the earth drinks the blood of an innocent victim, Abel. Clothing, initially sinful creatures' shameful response, becomes a sign of God's compassion. The developing history depicts divided peoples, both from the point of view of vocation (farmer, herdsman, musician, smith) and religion. Furthermore, the narrator tells of a weapon, the sword, and mentions migrations. In his view, the struggle to acquire economic security through civilization (culture) was accompanied by estrangement from God. The table of nations concedes that Israel was but one of many nations, a perennial problem for Yahwism. Still, one thing was absolutely certain: the tower of Babel represents the end of the road for the peoples who find themselves without an ounce of divine grace.[35]

In discussing the patriarchal narratives, von Rad stresses the means by which old stories were incorporated into Yahwistic traditions. The key to this recovery of earlier material resides in the idea of promise and fulfillment. Even the cult of the ancestors (the God of the ancestors, the Fear of Isaac, and the Mighty One of Jacob) was taken over, and these names became designations of Yahweh. Older narratives already contained the promise, according to von Rad, but this divine promise did not reckon with delayed fulfillment. In effect, the Egyptian interlude constituted a broken promise. The Yahwist took up these old narratives and united them around a twofold promise of land and progeny. Where stories contained no promise, as was the case with Genesis 22 (the offering of Isaac), Genesis 28, and the Joseph story (Gen. 37–50), he inserted the idea.

The priestly author associated the promise with Sinai, and widened its meaning. For him, the promise signified the origin of a people who enjoy a unique relationship with God, and to whom a land has been given. In Genesis 12–50 the promise sets in motion the whole saving history. Naturally, the promise encounters certain obstacles. Two receive considerable discussion: the problem of faith, and the hiddenness of God's actions. To recapitulate, old stories now refer to Israel's God, and give voice to her distinctive faith.

The confessional phrase *par excellence* in Israel was: "Yah-

weh brought us out of Egypt." The original setting of this confession must undoubtedly have been a hymn. Varying in length
from three words to extensive hymns, this confession proclaims
an event that actually happened, von Rad insists. Never for a
single moment did Israel spiritualize this event of the exodus.
Still, as the stories were handed on, the miraculous element increased markedly. Once the creation myth became attached to
the exodus event, a primeval dimension surfaced and the wondrous event was transferred from the realm of history. At that
moment, the story proclaims the beginning of Israel's existence.
The exodus was the creation of God's people.

For von Rad, redemption from Egypt includes the miracle at
the Reed Sea, the revelation of the name Yahweh, the revelation
at Sinai, and the story of wandering in the wilderness. Opting
for the meaning of Yahweh as presence ("I shall be present for
you"), he insists that Yahweh retained his freedom even when
disclosing the name. Von Rad notes that Israel's God has only
one name, whereas Marduk boasted fifty names. This name,
Yahweh, was not a possession of Israel to be used cavalierly;
care had to be taken lest the name fall into improper use.
Israel's sacred traditions posed a problem in regard to the name
of God, for a variety of names was actually preserved. One way
of dealing with this fact was to claim that Yahweh was unknown
until the revelation to Moses (Exod. 3). By this means, continuity in worship was maintained.

According to the priestly writer, Israel spent about a year at
Sinai, then went to Kadesh, from which spies were sent out to
determine the strength of the opposition. After an initial defeat,
Israel wandered for thirty-eight years. Once the older generation
had died, a second departure from Kadesh took place. The
people followed a strange route around Edom to the Dead Sea
and then northwards east of Jordan. The oldest story of this entry
into the promised land told of divine leading: Israel is silent,

and God acts. A tradition preserved in Jeremiah 2:1–3 accords with this positive understanding of Israel's first love. This interpretation stands in opposition to the dominant one, according to which the wilderness was a terrible ordeal that brought out the worst in Israel (Deut. 8:15–18; Ezek. 20; Ps. 78). For these later writers, the wilderness was characterized by constant murmuring.[36] Von Rad writes that the Hexateuch holds both views in tension. During this long experience God led his people and gave them various institutions as proof of his will to save. In addition, he fed Israel manna and quail, but in so doing God reminded the people of a need to rely wholly upon his leadership.[37]

With the settlement of the land, the sources of the Hexateuch come to an end. This occupation was accomplished largely without recourse to war, in von Rad's view; only later did the struggle with Canaanites erupt. The biblical story, on the other hand, emphasized the military victory over the inhabitants of the land. This account of a single conquest falls into the category of faith, not history. The traditions themselves refuse to allow such arbitrary treatment, von Rad argues. The result is a bundle of contradictions. Traditions from as late as the seventh century (a list of place names) put considerable strain on the account of the allocation of the land. In any event, these stories signal one fact: God has fulfilled all his promises.

DAVID AND ZION

Still, Israel's history opened up one further promise that became the next great focal point of Yahwistic thought. That divine word was proclaimed by the prophet Nathan, who spoke of Yahweh's establishing the Davidic dynasty for all time (2 Sam. 7). In Nathan's view, Yahweh endorsed the Davidic rule over Israel and guaranteed his throne forever. This promise was

interpreted anew by each generation. Von Rad recognizes in
this prophecy "the historical origin and legitimation of all
messianic expectations." [38]

We note a striking feature of this promise to David: it took
place after the king had moved to Jerusalem. To be sure,
David's "last words" in 2 Samuel 23:17 indicate that the ever-
lasting covenant with David is considerably older. Nevertheless,
the actual promise cannot be separated from a specific location
—Jerusalem (Zion). These two ideas, God's anointed ruler and
Zion, team up to create a living tradition with incredible power.
Their impact upon Israel's prophets and psalmists is discernible
at every stage of the tradition. Von Rad traces this powerful
tradition as manifest in the great historical works (the Succession Document, the Deuteronomistic history, the Chronicler),
certain Psalms, and prophetic literature.

Nathan's promise that a descendant of David would sit upon
the throne in Jerusalem gave birth to a belief that God would
deliver Jerusalem from all danger. Two stories dramatized
Yahweh's rescue of the holy city at the eleventh hour (2 Sam.
24; Isa. 36–37). Two prophets, Micah and Jeremiah, set themselves against this unconditional guarantee of protection, and
Ezekiel adopted an ambiguous stance toward a Davidic ruler.
Stark reality—that is, the fall of Jerusalem and disappearance
of the Davidic dynasty—evoked considerable questions about
God's faithfulness.

Two positive things came from this pathetic state in Jerusalem.
God's anointed was seen as one who suffers in behalf of others,
and a vision emerged of a new Zion over which God himself
would reign. Apocalyptic literature took up the latter vision and
by that means gave comfort to an oppressed people.[39]

III. Transmitters of Israel's Traditions

THE YAHWIST [1]

The theologian whom we call the Yahwist because of his prefer-
ence for the divine name Yahweh shaped the form of the Hexateuch more than any other person. His story of God's saving
activity runs from creation to the settlement by Israel in the
promised land. Von Rad writes that the Yahwist sought to lay
a foundation for God's kingdom on earth, and to lay it on the
bedrock of all human existence. It follows that von Rad rejects
the common notion of a Pentateuch, since these five books stop
short of the actual entrance into Canaan. Instead, he insists that
Joshua belongs to the first five books of the Bible, so that scholars are justified in speaking of a Hexateuch.

The inclusion of the Book of Joshua results in a welding together of sagas dealing with early history and Israel's specific
redemptive history. Von Rad thinks the Yahwist has brought
these two separate traditions together under a single theme: the

growing power of sin in the world. What was the nature of these
two literary complexes?

The patriarchal stories consisted of four cycles: (1) Abraham, (2) Isaac, (3) Jacob, (4) Joseph.[2] The Abraham saga
comprised two distinct cycles, one dealing with Abraham, and
another concerning Abraham and his nephew Lot. Two other
sagas treat Isaac. The Jacob tradition was woven from four
strands. The first discusses the conflicts between Jacob and Esau,
the second covers Jacob's dealings with Laban, the third includes some cultic sagas, and the fourth centers upon Jacob's
children. According to von Rad, the Joseph story demonstrates
the fact that the Yahwist functioned as a collector of traditions.
Still, the actual sequence represented in these sagas antedates
the Yahwist.

If the Yahwist is primarily a *collector* of patriarchal sagas,
what contribution did he make to them? Von Rad lists four
things that the Yahwist did in this regard: (1) he developed a
creedal deposit; (2) he ordered the distinct sagas to manifest
Yahweh's guidance in the entire story as well as in every single
episode within the greater literary complex; (3) he integrated
the sagas into the traditional notion of the God of the patriarchs
and the promise concerning the land, and (4) he reoriented the
sagas, so that they now introduce the settlement tradition.

Whence did the Yahwist derive an outline for this historical
work? Von Rad believes he discovered it in the settlement
tradition, which in turn evolved from the little historical creed.
In these credos (Deut. 26:5b–9; 6:20–24; Josh. 24:2–13), as
we have seen, Israel recalled her history from the patriarchal
journeyings, through Egyptian bondage, deliverance, and wan-
derings in the wilderness, to occupation of the land.

To these decisive moments in Israel's religious pilgrimage,
the Yahwist added an account of beginnings that placed Israel
in a world context. This prefixed primeval history made use of

copious materials that fell outside Israel's special history. In these old stories the Yahwist found a way to emphasize hidden grace alongside a widening gulf caused by sin. The result is what von Rad calls the aetiology of all Israelite aetiology. In these eleven chapters, the Yahwist traces the origins of the world and documents the spread of sin among God's creatures. God tries various ways of dealing with evil, but none succeeds.

Then God ventures forth in an entirely different direction. This bold plan is the Yahwist's free composition: God calls one man and intends to use him as a means of bringing blessing upon all the world. This new departure occurs in Genesis 12: 1–3.

> Now the Lord said to Abraham, "Go from your country and your kindred and your father's house to the land that I will show you. And I will make of you a great nation, and I will bless you, and make your name great, so that you will be a blessing. I will bless those who bless you, and him who curses you I will curse; and by you all the families of the earth will bless themselves."

One can view this passage as the Yahwist's confession that all previous attempts to eradicate sin had aborted. In his view, God had tried to discourage rebellion by direct prohibition, expulsion from the garden, withdrawal of his Spirit, and wholesale punishment. This poignant tale of divine struggle to overcome a powerful force teems with signs of grace despite a human inclination toward evil. God covered the first man and woman with an effective reminder that things have somehow gone awry, and he placed a protective mark on Cain, who had murdered his brother. When God finally determined to destroy humankind, he sought out and spared a righteous family lest the divine plan abort entirely. Even those who rebelled after the flood experienced God's compassionate response to heinous conduct and boundless pride. So the new thing in Genesis 12:1–3 does not concern a gracious turning toward mankind. Instead, it consists of God's election of one man through whom salvation will accrue to the whole world.

When is it likely that someone could have entertained such a grandiose conception of Israel's place within world history? Von Rad points to the untrammeled days of the Solomonic era as the probable date for the Yahwist's grand design of universal history. He strengthens his argument from several features of the Yahwistic narrative. In the first place, it manifests at most a tolerant stance over against the cult. Second, the promise has been fulfilled, for Israel has possession of the land. Third, God's hidden guidance of Israel continues into the present. Fourth, God's actions on his people's behalf take place outside sacral institutions, such as a holy sanctuary, or holy persons: Nazirite, prophet, charismatic leader. In von Rad's view, David's meteoric rise to power set into motion this new way of viewing God's activity in history. Von Rad emphasizes two basic facts: the new-found recognition of God's hidden activity in history and the relevance of ancient territorial claims to the time of David.

So far we have spoken of gospel only. Is there any place for law in the Hexateuch? Von Rad argues that the Yahwist incorporated the independent Sinai tradition into the settlement tradition, thereby joining together demand and grace. This remarkable blending of separate traditions gave definition to the two fundamental propositions of the Hebrew Bible: Law and Gospel.[3] According to covenantal traditions, including Yahweh's promise to the patriarchs and the settlement traditions, the initiative arose with Yahweh, and the active part of the saving drama was God's. On the contrary, in the Sinai tradition emphasis falls upon Israel's response to the divine command.

We branded the Yahwist a collector when dealing with the Joseph story. Was he more than that? Von Rad insists that "theologian" best describes this remarkable spokesman for Yahwistic traditions. Is it conceivable that the theory that grace coincided with rebellion belonged to the traditions which the Yahwist incorporated into a unified theology of world history? Von Rad denies any such theological tone to these patriarchal sagas in their original form. He writes: "The strong theological interest which gives cohesion to the Abraham sagas as we have them is certainly traceable to the Yahwist." Consequently, it is he who "postulates a hidden growth of grace alongside the ever-widening gulf between God and man." [4]

Not only was the Yahwist a theologian. He was also a skillful story teller. With matchless artistry, he weaves religious fantasy that captures the imagination. His stories bristle with bold anthropomorphisms, for he dares to depict God as acting in the manner of humans. This naïve depiction of God walking in the cool of a garden, for instance, is neutralized by rare psychological insight into the nature of human relations. Sophistication thus stands alongside simplicity, and both contribute to the impact of the narrative. All this adds up to the conclusion that the Yahwist was both a theologian and an author.

THE ELOHIST

Alongside the Yahwistic narrative stands another of equal narrative power, although existing only in torso. This tradition, which scholars call the Elohist, rarely occurs in the Hexateuch, but together with the Yahwistic source, gives final shape to the story of God's redemptive activity. Existing in purest form in the story of Abraham and Sarah in the territory of Abimelech of Gerar (Gen. 20) and the sacrifice of Isaac (Gen. 22),[5] this narrative complex stresses the ethical dimension of faith, emphasizes dreams, visions, and angels, and prefers the divine name *'elohim.*

THE DEUTERONOMIST

The years 722 and 587 B.C.E. brought an end to saving history in Israel and Judah respectively. The fall of Samaria to Assyria, followed by Jerusalem's surrender to Babylonia, marked a decisive stage in the history of God's dealing with his people.[6] Von Rad designates the age in which Deuteronomy [7] arose as the midpoint in the Old Testament. This book "wipes out some seven centuries squandered in disobedience, and places Israel once again in the wilderness, with Moses speaking to her." [8]

God's people finds itself once more on the road, staff in hand, poised to enter the promised land. Deuteronomy signals an interim period of saving history, the decisive age between election and fulfillment. The future is by no means assured; the book throbs with anxious feelings lest Israel scorn a marvelous opportunity to amend past ways. Von Rad underlines the novelty of this anxiety: "This is indeed something new—that disobedience with all its sinister possibilities has come within the range of Deuteronomy's theological vision." [9]

The fact that Israel exists in the space between election and fulfillment gives urgency to the message of the book. She must not choose death, when the offer of life opens up a wholly different alternative. Still, the book's message is couched in conditional terms. Israel may choose blessings or curses, which the author spells out in some detail. The contingent character of salvation exists in tension with Deuteronomy's insistence that God chose Israel in spite of her unworthiness. Inventing a new concept, that of election love, Deuteronomy compares God's love to a father's compassion for his son.

Eager to bestow his bounty upon obedient children, God promises blessing, land, and rest. The notion of divine blessing embraces the broad area normally attributed to Canaanite deities—fertility. God promises numerous children, rich harvests, and increase in flocks. Naturally, these blessings necessitate ample land; God therefore assures his people that they will inherit the land, which Deuteronomy praises as one flowing with milk and honey. Possessing riches and the good land, Israel will lack but one thing—rest. Defying active memory of invading troops year after year, the author of Deuteronomy dares to promise these products of an exhausted age that God will grant them rest from all their enemies.[10]

In form, Deuteronomy purports to be a speech by Moses. Through this literary fiction, the author manages to recreate the decisive stage in God's saving history and to pose the question of obedience once more. Accordingly, Moses summons Israel to obedience; in doing so, he warns of terrible dangers and offers rich rewards in God's name. The law of God itself assumes hortatory form: Moses preaches *the torah*. Von Rad observes that this understanding of God's entire revelation as a unity, the totality of teaching, is entirely new. On the basis of an allusion in Nehemiah 8:7–8 to preachers of the law, he suggests that there must have been an office of law preacher in ancient Israel.

While the law is a unity, it was not communicated on a single occasion. Moses delivered the Decalogue from Sinai at an earlier time; now he proclaims the complete law for God's people. Von Rad distinguishes several stages in the laws preserved in Deuteronomy. He thinks it is possible to discover the earliest laws, both in terms of form and content. Comparison of Deuteronomic laws with those making up the Holiness Code (Lev. 17–26) leads him to the position that Deuteronomy has the purer form.

The attempted balance between grace and demand tips in favor of law, particularly in the later additions to Deuteronomy. Von Rad writes that Deuteronomy elevates law over gospel. However, he later modifies that position by arguing that election

precedes obedience. "It is therefore quite impossible to understand the commandments in Deuteronomy as 'law' in the theological sense of the word, as though Deuteronomy were leading
Israel to earn salvation by a total obedience." [11]

Moses' speech bristles with polemic. Israel found herself in
a precarious political situation, threatened on every hand by
surrounding peoples. Her survival lay in the balances, neces-
sitating Deuteronomy's bold bid for unification by means of a
national community (God's people). The Canaanite nature
religion poses a dangerous threat; to combat it, Deuteronomy
revives an earlier institution, that of holy war. Even in the important account of speeches associated with Yahweh's wars, the
critic can recognize three stages. Harking back to the amphictyony at Shechem, Deuteronomy preserves theological views
connected with the ark.

Von Rad lays great emphasis upon Deuteronomy's theology
of the name. God promises to make his name dwell with his holy
people. That name will take up residence in the one place God
chooses, usually designated by the adverb *there*. Originally this
word referred to Shechem, but now it unmistakably alludes to
Jerusalem.

Since Israel is a unity, it follows that she has one God, one
revelation, one cult, one land, one worship place, and one
prophet. How easily Deuteronomy solves the vexing problem of
false prophecy! [12] Von Rad recognizes the simplistic reasoning
that accompanies such emphasis upon unification. Even if partly
attributable to rhetoric, such lack of realism scarcely took seri-
ously the truth residing in alternative views. The priestly author's tent of meeting as the place at which Israel encountered
God's glory, a view which Deuteronomy flatly repudiates, was
fraught with fewer problems, in my view, than the theology of
presence Deuteronomy adopted. The latter theology of the ark

was faced with serious consequences when God withdrew from his people, which unfortunately he often did.

Precisely who instituted this revival movement in ancient Israel? Von Rad identifies their self portrait in Deuteronomy 20. Since only priests had access to such legal materials as Deuteronomy introduces, and owned the exclusive right to reinterpret such legislation, we must look to them. But how can we explain the martial spirit characterizing the book? Von Rad conjectures that the people of the land preserved the old patriarchal traditions and treasured certain amphictyonic principles. The surrender of Judah's militia in 701 B.C.E. forced the population at large to muster an army to combat enemy invasion. The people of the land supported Joash, Josiah, and Jehoahaz —that is, those kings who had participated in efforts to revive an earlier way of life. These people of the land, *'am ha-'arets*, reached a compromise position between two opposing views: David's centrality and the restoration of the amphictyony. Retaining a king, Deuteronomy subjects him to Yahweh's law. Such purely parenetic "laws" arose concerning prophets, cities of refuge, defection to idolatry, and divination.

Who were the spokesmen for this revivalistic group, the people of the land? Von Rad suggests that Levites assumed this important role. Since they were priests, the Levites had access to legal materials; at the same time, they may have been relegated to a teaching function prior to this time, and thus brought long experience in rhetoric to bear upon the new bid for unification. Von Rad insists that the traditions preserved in Deuteronomy derive from the North, rather than from Judah. The demand for centralization of worship at one sanctuary, it follows, arose at a later time and distorts the original purpose of the book. One can hardly suppose that Levites supported a principle which worked against their own best interests.

The Deuteronomistic history seized this demand for a central cult and used it as a standard by which to assess the complete history of Israel and Judah. The purity of Yahweh's cult at Jerusalem thus constituted proof of religious integrity for this author. In this way, the Deuteronomistic history interprets the course of political events as God's fulfilling of his word. The long history of failure ends on a positive note, von Rad claims, for it refers to a release of King Jehoiachin from captivity.[13] Once again God's people has reason to hope that the old promises will finally materialize, and a descendant of David, the king after God's own heart, will rule in the city where God's name dwells.

THE DEUTERONOMISTIC HISTORIAN

Standing in the shadow of two great calamities, the collapse of Israel and Judah, the Deuteronomistic historian [14] sought to understand how God could reject his people. Had he proved unfaithful? On the contrary, God had exercised infinite patience with his people, but had now finally allowed the cumulative weight of sin to fall upon one and all. Von Rad describes the Deuteronomistic historical work as "a great 'doxology of judgment' transferred from the cultic to the literary sphere." In another context he characterizes the work as a "comprehensive confession of Israel's guilt." [15] Here we encounter the first clearly formulated discussion of the phenomenon called saving history.

In this account of salvation history, a clear structure bestows unity upon disparate traditions. The operation of the prophetic word in effecting destruction and well-being comprises this peculiar theological framework. Attempting to embrace all of history, the Deuteronomistic history emphasizes Israel's waywardness and vulnerability over against nature religions. The choice between Yahwism and this tempting alternative stands as a *status confessionis* in this Deuteronomistic attempt to wrestle with the burden of solidified past history.

Earlier stories provided the materials from which the author composed his sweeping judgment of Israel's past actions. Here and there, he injected his own free renderings (for example, 2 Kings 17:7–18). In von Rad's view, differences between the stories in Judges and those in Kings suggest different hands. In the former book, a cyclical understanding of history unfolds: the people sin, Yahweh punishes them by means of neighboring powers, they repent, and God delivers them from distress. In these stories, the charismatic leaders fall away from their high calling, and Yahweh alone achieves salvation. Von Rad notes that a pessimistic mood characterizes these stories, since human leaders invariably fail. Interestingly, these narratives think charismatic rule is more appropriate for Israel than the monarchy.

In Kings the destructive force stays its hand while sin mounts, eventually falling upon Israel in 722 B.C.E. and Judah in 587 B.C.E. According to von Rad, a great gulf exists between the end of Judges and the point at which the Deuteronomistic historian inserts his views. From 1 Samuel 13 to 1 Kings 3, that is, the specific characteristics of the Deuteronomistic history do not occur. The very human David who appears in the Succession Document, for example, has little in common with the ideal David so dear to the Deuteronomistic historian.

That leads us to a further feature of the work under consideration. According to the Deuteronomistic history, kings are the object of the prophetic word, since the people rise or fall with their ruler. In this regard, Judges once again differs from Kings, for in these old narratives of individual judges the decisions of the people actively shape their future.

Von Rad regards the major problem of the Deuteronomistic

history as the correlation of Moses and David. Yahweh's word becomes the primary concern of his ruler, who is responsible for implementing that word in the life of the nation. In short, the law of Moses is entrusted to the king. Von Rad insists that the torah comprises both law and gospel. As law, it effects punishment for transgression, and as gospel, it brings well-being.

While the Deuteronomistic historian devoted considerable time to documenting the punitive aspect of the prophetic word, he does not stop with discussion of threats and their fulfillment. Instead, he envisions an infinitely patient God who eagerly promises blessings for those who pay heed to the divine word. This desire to bless his people finds expression in Nathan's prophecy to David that God would establish a permanent Davidic dynasty in the Holy City.

This hope appeals to the heart of the Israelites, and has absolutely nothing to do with the cultic realm. Prayer functions as the means to God's promises, and individual choice faces everyone. Curiously, kings, upon whom the peoples' fate depends, are censured by the Deuteronomistic historian, whereas the judges escape censure altogether. Von Rad believes the ending of the Deuteronomistic work points to a possible restoration of the Davidic monarchy, inasmuch as King Jehoiachin has been set free.

THE PRIESTLY DOCUMENT

We must recognize the historical character of the priestly document,[16] despite its appearance to the contrary. This work endeavors to offer legitimation for Israel's various priestly offices and rites. Its subject matter, then, consists of whatever goes into Israel's cultic institutions. The author traces the growth of the institutional cult within Israel's peculiar saving history. He focuses upon the institutions of circumcision and passover, and emphasizes the special status assigned to Aaron and the Levites.

In contrast to Deuteronomy, this author adopts a style that gives the appearance of bare objective reporting. Whereas the author of Deuteronomy spoke to the heart, the priestly writer addresses himself to the intellect—if one is permitted to use a distinction that did not apply in the Old Testament. Von Rad characterizes the priestly document as verbose, stiff, and cold. Perhaps "tedious" best describes the long genealogies, extravagant detail, and constant repetition that marks this priestly work.

We have said that the priestly author appealed to the mind, but it must be granted that he neglects significant issues like the theological meaning of various institutions. In addition, he does not attempt to justify the choice of circumcision, for example, as the special sign of God's people. It seems not to have occurred to him that another mark might have functioned just as well. Nor does he seek to justify the prerogative granted priests and Levites, a status that was far from self-evident.

The priestly history of cultic institutions is by no means a complete theology of Israel's cult. Instead, it takes much for granted, and seems content merely to trace the emergence of certain cherished cultic rites and the officials responsible for them. Like Deuteronomy, it stands upon a Sinaitic base, attempting to come to grips with revelation at Sinai. However, unlike Deuteronomy, the priestly work preserves Judean, that is, southern, traditions. Of course it contains numerous materials that derive from considerably earlier periods than the actual date of the priestly author (perhaps fifth century).

Precisely what was the nature of these ancient materials? The old traditions about a tent of meeting and an ark depicting divine presence merge in the priestly author. Two mutually contradictory ideas about God's means of encountering Israel

are thus brought together. According to the old tradition of the
tent, God came down to meet his chosen representative and
to declare his will for the people, but his dwelling was in
heaven. The ark symbolizes that presence. The priestly author
brings the two ideas together with the notion of a holy tabernacle. Here God dwelt in supreme holiness.

The priestly term for God's self-manifestation, *glory,* carries
the basic idea of weightiness. A person's glory consists of that
which makes him or her impressive. Both in Ezekiel and in the
priestly writing, the glory of God comprises a technical term to
describe theophanies.

Because God manifested himself to Israel on solemn occasions, care had to be taken lest he be offended. The function
of priestly orders was aimed at preparing the people for this
awesome confrontation. Specialists in distinguishing the sacred
from the profane, these priests engaged in a rigorous intellectual
enterprise.

According to von Rad, their task embraced far more than
the offering of various sacrifices. Instead, they answered all
sorts of questions concerning things clean and unclean, as well
as rendering decisions relating to sacral procedure. In addition,
they carried on a teaching ministry, and collected decisions in
cultic matters, from which no appeal could be made. Perhaps
their most significant contribution to Israel's worship fell in the
area of liturgical composition. Israel's priests wrote the many
liturgies that were then recited by pilgrims who attended the
various sacred festivals. With so much power in their hands, it
is surprising, according to von Rad, that these priests never developed powerful hierarchies. Instead, they busied themselves
with more important things than the acquisition of power.

In the priestly terminology, the closest thing to a term desig-
nating one's full obligation consisted of the expression, "for
Yahweh." Everything offered up or performed carried one

motivation—to be "for the Lord." Inasmuch as sin and guilt
existed as an objective reality, expiation by means of sin offerings was absolutely essential to the well-being of God's people.
The priestly writer seems to assume that an objective wrath
hovers over Israel constantly, and this divine anger must be
placated lest it break forth destructively.

Two areas that presented special danger were sex and things
ritually unclean. Priests devoted a major portion of their time
addressing these important matters and attempting to prepare
persons for divine encounter. Appearing before God in a state
of ritual uncleanliness placed a person in grave danger. Ignorance was no excuse in God's sight.

As is well known, the priestly writer attempted to depict
Israel's saving history as a series of divine manifestations. Three
decisive events stand out: the appearances to Noah, Abraham,
and Moses. In each instance, God entered into a covenant relationship and granted signs as constant reminders of the bond
established in this encounter. Accordingly, the rainbow, circumcision, and the Decalogue function to remind all mankind in
Noah's case, and Israel in the other two instances, of God's self-
manifestation.

In truth, the essential role of priests, according to the priestly
author, was that of bringing Israel to God's remembrance. In
everything that these holy persons did, they hoped to bring the
people to God's mind and to dispose him favorably to his own
children. Von Rad insists that these priests did not lack a vision
of the full achieving of God's will. In their hopes and dreams,
they anticipated an age in which God would dwell among his
people, who would reflect his will fully in their daily activities.

Until that time, Israel's priests summoned the people to appropriate silence in God's presence. In the priestly document,
God's right to men and women's complete surrender elicits
silence before him, and evokes the refrain: "Silence (*has*) at

the presence of Yahweh. Silence at the presence of Yahweh! He rouses himself from his holy dwelling." [17]

To summarize: the priestly author wrote a history of Israel's cultic institutions. In his view, it was no exaggeration to understand the Israelite cult established at Sinai as the goal toward which creation itself pointed.

THE CHRONICLER

Whereas the Deuteronomistic historian had composed a great theology of sin and guilt, the Chronicler created a theology of praise.[18] His miserable political situation notwithstanding, this author of lavish praise expressed unlimited self-confidence. Indeed, he viewed the whole course of human history from Adam to his own day (approximately 400 B.C.E.) as having taken place for Israel's own sake.

Dependent upon Deuteronomy's preaching style and the literary base provided by the Deuteronomistic history, the Chronicler worked this material over in an arbitrary manner. Whereas the Deuteronomist had retained a concept of history as a unity despite his theory of sin and punishment, the Chronicler lost sight of this important understanding of historical unity. Attempting a complete rational proof for every disaster, he sought to demonstrate that there was no sin without punishment.

This conviction prompted him to take considerable liberty with history as he received it. For instance, the king who reigned longest in Israel, Manasseh, posed cogent evidence that God did not in fact punish all evil men, since his pagan practices were well known. To combat this embarrassing example, the Chronicler fabricated an account of the king's repentance and minor cultic reform, for which God naturally rewarded him. In the Chronicler's view, each individual generation rose or fell with its anointed one. Von Rad accuses the Chronicler of mental exhaustion, particularly because of a lack of clarity and theological unity.

The Chronicler's tendency to cover up the mistakes of its heroes, David in particular, provokes von Rad's strong criticism: "Certainly, what is most serious of all is the denial of the realities of human life, the 'extent [to which] the veil is drawn over the scandalous falls of saints.' " [19] Nevertheless, he remarks that a work so full of praise can hardly be far off target.

It has been said that history for the Chronicler begins with David. All history before him is a prelude. This king after God's own heart gives the appearance of a spotless holy one who delivers solemn orations. David's great contribution fell in the area of Israel's cult: he instigated the building of the temple, furnishing Solomon with an exact pattern for it just as Moses had done for the Tabernacle. In addition, David instituted the musical guild connected with the Temple, and called upon the people to perform certain sacrifices.

With this mention of David we have arrived at the Chronicler's real purpose in adapting Deuteronomistic traditions to his own time: he sought to legitimate the cultic offices that David founded. In truth, the Chronicler became a spokesman for the Levitical temple singers.

In the work of the Chronicler, von Rad discovers a new literary form, the Levitical sermon. According to him, the speeches cite earlier prophetic words and offer theological retrospect about national history. Here Israel's king dons the garb of preacher; at times it seems as if the Chronicler falls into a sermonic style by mistake. These sermons consist of doctrine, application, and exhortation, but are, strictly speaking, not really prophetic.

Most astonishingly, the sermon mentions belief in Yahweh and his prophets in the same sentence. Never before had one dared speak in such a fashion. Von Rad thinks ritual (the letter

of the law) has taken precedence in Chronicles. To this late
author election signified God's choice of a king, a cultic center,
and the tribe of Levi. For others, it referred to God's selection
of the people Israel. From these delineations of the meaning of
election in Chronicles, von Rad concludes that covenant theology
is wholly lacking in this Levitical spokesman.

The tendency of Chronicles to quote earlier written sources,
von Rad writes, signals a declension in religious vigor and spon-
taneity. On the other hand, from the fact that the sources are not
cited, he concludes that they must not have been considered
sacred. Although the Chronicler gives the impression that the
letter of the law had stifled its spirit, that is not exactly the case.
Von Rad refuses to label Chronicles "narrow legalism," noting
the paradox that praise and faith arise from the pen of Israel's
officials.

If we ask what special function the Chronicler performed in
his own way, we might wish to answer that "in his miserable
age when there were no kings, the Chronicler is the guardian of
the messianic tradition." [20] In majestic fashion, he raises David
above the level of ordinary men. Justification for such elevation
he would certainly have found in the fact that God chose David
to be his special anointed one.

PROPHETS

According to Jeremiah 18:18, three institutions existed in
Israel, each with its special concern. Prophets uttered a word,[21]
priests dispersed torah, and sages gave counsel. We turn now
to examine the first of these three. In doing so, we shall ask the
following question: What was the essence of prophecy? Were
all prophets alike? To whom did they speak? What traditions
did individual prophets proclaim? What validated their mes-

sage? Was prophecy a lifelong vocation? Did their calling do away with personal freedom? What hope enabled them to endure opposition from various quarters? Do prophets have anything in common with apocalyptists?

Nineteenth-century critics *discovered* prophecy, long neglected in the writings of Christian theologians. To men like Wellhausen and Bernard Duhm, who is best known for his hypothesis that the servant poems in Second Isaiah form a separate unit within that book, as well as for his valuable commentaries on Jeremiah and Isaiah,[22] the prophets had direct access to God. As a consequence, they achieved ethical monotheism, Israel's great contribution to religious thought. Naturally, such elevation of prophecy came at the law's expense, and has been discredited by contemporary research.[23]

Now if we cannot single out prophecy for its immediate access to God, and consequently for truth that transcends historical limitations, what was the essence of that remarkable phenomenon in Israel? In von Rad's view, a prophet was a bearer of tradition and an intercessor. The first aspect of prophecy focuses upon the past, while the second concentrates on the vulnerable present. Standing at a decisive turning point in history, each prophet endeavored to actualize ancient traditions in new settings and forms.

Prophets were extraordinary figures, for God called them to their task. Von Rad understands the call narratives as public validation; by writing down these individual reports of divine summons, prophets sought to achieve credentials that would enable them to function freely. Obviously, false prophets could fabricate accounts of their call, so that in the final analysis certification lacked persuasive power.[24] In this regard, von Rad endeavored to comprehend the perplexing issue of false prophecy by adopting a historical criterion. Unfortunately, the problem is far too complex to solve in this fashion. False prophets could also interpret history as the scene within which God performed redemptive acts.

Because prophets felt God's hand upon them, they entered into his service and proclaimed his word vouchsafed to them. In effect, they did enjoy immediate access to God through his council, but this privilege hardly provided any comfort. Instead, it introduced prophets to God's psyche, as Abraham Heschel saw with exceptional clarity.[25] As a result, prophets shared God's pathos, and sought to communicate the intensity of God's feelings to a people who seemed to have lost all capacity to feel.

In addition to being called and sharing God's pathos, prophets were interpreters of God's word to the people. To understand prophecy correctly, von Rad observes, one must be conscious of the correlation between word and history and the prophetic movement. Israel's prophets viewed historical events as actualization of the divine Word. By piling together a whole series of episodes in which God's deed was manifest, these prophets achieved an astonishing breakthrough: they discovered linear time as opposed to cyclical time. The numerous manifestations of God's word demonstrated progress toward a distant mark. But gaps occurred in that onward march, and at times prophets reversed earlier words completely.

So far, we have spoken as if all prophets were alike. This is far from the case. Israel's earliest prophets, Elijah and Elisha especially, seem to have understood themselves as bearers of the spirit rather than the word. Here von Rad agrees with the thesis first advanced by the great Scandinavian literary critic, Sigmund Mowinckel, whose interpretation of the psalms in light of a royal enthronement ceremony is well known.[26] Emphasis falls upon the prophetic deed instead of his message. Von Rad distinguishes carefully between the Elijah stories, in which God is the true subject, and the Elisha narrative, where the miracle-working prophet appears as the hero. Perhaps, von Rad conjectures, northern prophecy stressed God's spirit while prophecy in Judah emphasized the word.

We must be careful not to minimize the spiritual quality of certain Elijah and Elisha episodes. Following a clue furnished by Alt,[27] von Rad interprets the confrontation between Elijah and Baal prophets on Mount Carmel as restoration of a Yahwistic outpost in pagan territory. Von Rad thinks the historical kernel of the story is the likelihood that Elijah forced Israel's authorities to take action against religious syncretism. Whereas the simple folk preserved pure Yahweh worship, upper classes and members of the court served Yahweh and Baal. Incidentally, Elijah's slaughter of Baal's prophets was not motivated by vengeance, but was dictated by the ancient amphictyonic curse on an idolater.

The majestic account of a theophany at Horeb, von Rad insists, does not contain an implicit attack against phenomena of the spirit such as fire, wind, and earthquake. On the contrary, it endorses Elijah's zeal for the Lord. The point of the story is God's word, here a small whisper. But that still voice spoke a horrendous message, one that was absolutely new: God might resolve to destroy Israel, leaving only a remnant. This is surely the point of the reference to seven thousand people who have not betrayed the Lord.

Although von Rad views the Elisha narrative from a negative standpoint, he manages to salvage one important episode—the healing of Naaman the Syrian. In this beautiful story, two high points stand on each side of the rather incidental report of a healing. On the one side, we have a confrontation between Elisha and a Syrian, who expects all sorts of hocus-pocus and is greatly disappointed. On the other side, we see Elisha's extraordinary pastoral role. When asked whether Naaman can transport some dirt from the land over which Yahweh ruled, the prophet gave his permission. Behind this request lay a fear that leprosy would return once Naaman left territory ruled over by Israel's powerful God. Naaman's second request concerns mental reservation: will he be permitted to carry out his task as a military captain in Syria, bowing before foreign gods while actually serving Yahweh? Elisha's response demonstrates amazing tolerance: "Go in peace."

According to 1 Samuel 9:9, the ancient seer evolved into a *nabi'*, the usual term for prophet in later Israel. Von Rad writes that we lack sufficient data to judge the reliability of this bit of information. On the surface, at least, a shift in emphasis did take place. Early prophecy stressed wondrous deeds, while subsequent prophets emphasized their message from God. Even this description of the situation may falsify, inasmuch as certain late texts describe Isaiah as a miracle worker comparable to Elisha.[28] In addition, later prophets like Jeremiah, Second Isaiah, and the author of the Servant Poems, scarcely made a distinction between the prophetic word and their office. Instead, God's word is fully internalized. Thus Jeremiah eats the word, and finds it to be sweet as honey. Ezekiel, too, devours a scroll, which is a symbolic way of saying that he internalized his message.

Ancient seers often worked in conjunction with cultic centers. In effect, they were cultic officials. Can we say the same for Israel's prophets? Von Rad grants that possibility for Nahum only; none of the others had any vital connection with Israel's cult. Proof for this position comes from several directions: the existence of prophetesses, which is inconceivable if prophets belonged to cultic centers;[29] the overwhelmingly judgmental tone of their message; the fact that prophets were called to their task; and the devastatingly minimal effect of their work. Von Rad insists that cultic prophets necessarily proclaimed well-being, and that the cult implied at least some success for its very existence. In addition, true prophets did not choose their vocation, which was thrust upon them from above.

A decisive shift took place when collective thinking began to break down. Prophets suddenly confront the vexing problem of God's justice and make frequent use of I-Thou language. It would be wrong, however, to assume that early prophets lost their personal identity in the larger group. On the contrary, individual pathos erupts now and again in the great eighth-century prophets Amos, Hosea, and Isaiah. Nevertheless, the pastoral function certainly occupies a larger place in Ezekiel's ministry than in that of Amos or Isaiah, who spoke almost exclusively about God's judgment upon the sinful people.

To whom did prophets address themselves? Not all of the recorded words spoke to the same people. In fact, von Rad believes that certain hopeful descriptions of a coming ruler were addressed to Isaiah's intimate disciples and were never intended for a wider public. In accepting the hypothesis of prophetic disciples, first proposed by Mowinckel as a clue to understanding the preservation of the prophetic tradition,[30] von Rad opens up the difficult task of distinguishing which texts were intended for wider dissemination. One means of achieving this goal is to determine specific rhetorical features that seem best suited to the people in general. Von Rad calls attention to *ad hominem* arguments within prophetic oracles, as well as to symbolic actions.[31] The latter feature of prophecy depends upon the magical power inherent within ritual. Symbolic actions constitute an intensified form of speech, one which was believed to have set into motion that to which it pointed.

Above all else, von Rad views the prophets from the point of view of the traditions that they acknowledge in one way or another. He recognizes a period during which prophetic material circulated orally, at first in story form, and later actual collections of *logia*, that is, prophetic oracles. Strictly speaking, a

prophetic oracle consists of a messenger formula ("Thus has
Yahweh spoken" or "oracle of the Lord") plus diatribe (threat)
or exhortation. In time, separate units were gathered into small
complexes (for example, the oracles against prophets in Jeremiah 23:9–40 or the messianic oracles in Isaiah 6:1–9:7).
Editorial connections mark the next stage when larger complexes
were brought together; such signs of editing include catchwords,
chronological observations, and individual topics of special
interest.

Israel's prophets did not live in a vacuum. They borrowed
literary forms from every area of life (hymns, popular songs,
funeral laments, wisdom sayings, and so forth). The form in
which a prophetic word appeared is important; form and content are inseparable. It follows that adoption of literary features
from external sources gave new content to the prophetic word.
Still, the traditions from which each prophet lived gave final
shape to the message.

The prophet Amos took his stand solidly upon the Davidic
and Zion traditions. Only a faint "perhaps" left a door open
to hope that God would not utterly destroy his people. Ex-
pressing himself in diatribes against a people who showed con-
tempt for Yahweh's law and lolled in religious complacency
while poor people starved, Amos pronounced a terrible threat
upon the whole nation. Nevertheless, von Rad writes, the prophet
was Judean in origin, and consequently he shared the hoped for
restoration that now concludes the book that goes by his name.

Both Hosea and Jeremiah took up Israel's election traditions
(exodus, covenant, conquest). The former illustrated his message
by marrying a wayward woman, who enacted the behavior of
Israel and Judah. Since Hosea's much discussed marriage was
a symbolic act, it tells modern interpreters next to nothing about
his own domestic situation.[32] The point of his marriage is simple:

Yahweh will take Israel back to the beginning once more, wiping out a history of sinfulness.

In his early ministry, Jeremiah owes much to Hosea. Surprisingly, he turned his back upon the Zion tradition, and like Micah before him, announced the downfall of the Jerusalem temple. Von Rad thinks God led Jeremiah step by step into the terrifying darkness of God-forsakenness.

We are indebted to Isaiah for preservation of the Zion tradition. In his thinking, God stood ready to deliver a beseiged Jerusalem at the eleventh hour. Unfortunately, von Rad concedes, not a single one of Isaiah's messages about God's deliverance of Zion came true. One would think such a poor track record at prediction would have discredited the prophet. We must remember that every prophetic word is contingent upon the response accorded it. To be effectual, promises must give birth to appropriate action, just as threats that evoke genuine repentance may abort.

This contingent character of prophecy appears most clearly in the didactic Book of Jonah. Von Rad refuses to acknowledge any universalistic tendency in this fictional account of a pitiful prophetic figure whose chief folly was aloofness. Since God cared what happened to all of his creatures, the prophet worthy of his calling must do likewise—even at the expense of personal reputation for accuracy in predicting future events.

Isaiah, too, underlines the importance of human response in his familiar promise to King Ahaz that a young woman would soon give birth to a wondrous son whose name would be "God with us." Because of the people's refusal to heed his message, Isaiah seized the old tradition about divine hardening of human hearts and made effective use of it. Still, Isaiah walked a tight rope, due largely to his great respect for Amos's message of judgment on the one hand, and his conviction that Yahweh would engage in holy war on behalf of his people, on the other hand. Occasionally, the tension became more than he could bear. The result was an eruption of human feelings.

> Therefore I said:
> "Look away from me,
>   let me weep bitter tears;
> do not labor to comfort me
>   for the destruction of the daughter of my people" (22:4).

Such personal expressions detract little if any from Isaiah's total message, which achieves the theological high watermark in ancient Israel.

So far I have said nothing about Isaiah's relationship to historical events that swept Israel along like a straw in flood waters. Von Rad notes that Isaiah's prophetic activity revolved around three political events, all of which constituted rebellion against the power of Assyria: Hamath and Hanun of Gaza in 720 B.C.E.; the Ashdod rebellion in 713–711, in which Hezekiah participated; and the Askelon rebellion in 705, involving Judah.[33] Essentially, Isaiah's activity was limited to these three periods. Von Rad thus does not view prophecy as a permanent vocation, except in Jeremiah's case. In this regard, he argues that Amos probably returned to Judah after being advised to do so by Amaziah, and that he then resumed his earlier way of life.

The prophet Ezekiel was a theologian as well; more than any other prophet, he thinks out the complexities of theological problems. Unable to expound the David tradition, Ezekiel renews the old Sinai tradition. Accordingly, he emphasizes God's honor and name. For Ezekiel, sin was a sacral offense, and the prophet functioned as a watchman over Israel. Pressing individualism to the extreme, he insisted that life would not balance out so that a preponderance of good over evil would count in one's favor.

Others had viewed Israel's history positively, although Amos

had dared to parody sacred recitation of God's saving deeds
(4:6–11). Von Rad writes that Ezekiel turns history into a
monstrous thing. Judah and Israel sinned from the beginning. To
illustrate this propensity toward unfaithfulness, Ezekiel describes the two kingdoms as two harlot sisters who wage battle
to see which one can be more profligate.

Despite his pessimistic view of history, Ezekiel nurtured
strong hope for restoration. His own symbolic actions portrayed
the agony through which God's people must pass before the
spirit gives new life to dry bones. In this powerful vision of the
rebirth of a nation (ch. 37), Ezekiel proclaims his unshakable
conviction that God will cause all people to know that he is Lord.
Naturally, the description of a restored community (chs. 40–44)
accompanies such faith.

This brief account of the traditions which individual prophets
inherited suffices to indicate the nature of von Rad's analysis of
the several prophetic books. From one perspective, his treatment
of prophecy overlooks significant themes that cannot easily be
subsumed under one of the chief historical traditions that mean
so much to von Rad. In truth, one can easily fault him for ignoring many important features of prophecy.[34] Still, what he does
discuss illuminates the prophetic literature again and again,
often where more traditional approaches have yielded meager
results.

Von Rad's particular approach poses a special problem in
another respect. If prophets functioned in the service of tradition, what becomes of their freedom? Von Rad's answer concentrates on the call narratives, where Isaiah and Jeremiah
freely offer themselves in God's service. This total surrender,
von Rad insists, constitutes true freedom.

Perhaps we have further access to a prophet's freedom in the
way he handled revered traditions. If so, we are not limited to
the initial decision that sprang from free choice, but can look

for examples of free thinking throughout the prophet's ministry. Each prophet interpreted God's will in terms of past tradition and the historical hour in which he or she lived. In one area that personal freedom approaches defiance of God, but this rebellion takes its stand upon God's compassion.

I have reference to the prophetic hope for Israel in the face of continued rebellion. Certainty that God's promises were trustworthy, regardless of Israel's recalcitrance, led the prophets to develop a sure hope that God would establish his kingdom in the latter days. This expectation was grounded in the glory of God, not in human accomplishments.

Precisely at this point prophecy and apocalyptic converge. Both think in terms of a decisive act of God, for which the people eagerly wait. Essential differences exist, however, for prophets envision God attacking his own people. Von Rad thinks that the historical view in apocalyptic has more in common with wisdom than with prophecy. In particular, he specifies an absence of any existential relationship with history in apocalyptic. Instead, one reads about knowledge as the nerve center, and emphasis is placed on secret times.

Just what is this phenomenon called apocalyptic? [35] Von Rad stresses the following identifying marks: eschatological dualism, sheer transcendentalism, pseudonymity, esotericism, and gnosticism. He writes that Daniel's universalistic view of history leaves no room for Israelite sacred history except for the last generation. Furthermore, his understanding of history lacks movement. As such, it veils the point in time at which the word emerged. Rejecting the Maccabean dating of the early stories in Daniel, von Rad observes that passive resistence does not suit that age. He naturally considers the allusion to Antiochus Epiphanes a later addition to the book.

If we ask what contribution prophecy made to Israel's religious development, one way of answering our question is to concentrate on the new elements in eighth-century prophecy, which stands as the pinnacle of prophetic thought. Von Rad singles out four things: (1) they summoned Israel before Yahweh's judgment seat as one who has already been condemned; (2) they endeavored to comprehend Israel's conduct in its entirety; (3) they pronounced the verdict that Israel's history had failed; and (4) they announced that future acts alone signaled salvation for Israel.

This new prophetic tradition constantly took new shape, for it was living reality to many faithful followers of the great prophets. Second Isaiah furnishes evidence that Isaiah's message bore rich fruit. In his case, the messenger hides behind the message, which reaffirms the old exodus, David, and Zion traditions. To these election themes he added the creation tradition, while democratizing the David tradition and thus robbing it of content. A new redemptive act awaits on the horizon, one that completely dwarfs all previous saving events. Yahweh stands ready to accompany his people on a newly formed highway through the desert. God's dealings with Israel have thus come full circle: "Forget the past," this poet cries. Here hymnic diction clothes the message appropriately, and prophecy embraces praise. Only to a point, however, for awe takes over when the poet moves to speak about the means by which salvation will be accomplished. The servant of the Lord will offer his life for others.

SAGES

The text from which we began our analysis of Israelite prophecy also refers to sages who give counsel (Jer. 18:18). Von Rad's major study of wisdom in Israel stands as a monument to his extraordinary powers of interpretation.[36] It also demonstrates his willingness to adopt a different approach when the literature demands it.

Von Rad's departure from tradition history in favor of problem history is an endeavor to understand both the religious tensions that brought various texts to life, as well as the thematic concerns of the sages. Still, von Rad remarks that the sages' teachings about a self-manifesting created order comprise a model of transmitted traditions. In examining those texts which refer to personified wisdom (Prov. 8; Job 28; Ecclus. 24; Wisd. of Sol. 8), von Rad seems very much at home. Here a specific tradition assumes slightly different configurations as it develops from personification to actual hypostasis (a manifestation of a divine attribute, in this instance wisdom).

Who were these sages, and where did they function?[37] Von Rad opts for a court setting, and posits a school after the pattern of Egypt and Mesopotamia. Besides the analogy with sages in neighboring environs, he thinks the quality of literature produced by the wise and the rhetorical devices they employ demand a school context. In particular, he mentions certain passages that resemble school questions, as well as catechetical texts.

Analogy with neighboring great powers convinced von Rad that Israel's kings would have needed a sufficient number of trained officials to justify court schools. When this projected need is coupled with narrative accounts of royal counselors, such as Ahithophel and Hushai, von Rad believes the hypothesis of an Israelite school makes sense long before the first reference to a house of learning by Sirach. Von Rad is troubled by the paucity of proverbs that derive from or apply to a courtly setting, but tries to diminish the impact of this fact by appealing to the general character of wisdom, which addresses itself to all people. Still, he admits that the proverbs lack a bureaucratic ethic,[38] which scribes training for court service would certainly require. A single glance at Egyptian wisdom suffices to make this point tellingly. Interestingly, von Rad locates much of the wisdom literature in landed estates. Presumably, these relatively affluent citizens alone had the education and leisure to study.[39]

Von Rad's analysis of the literary forms used by the sages breaks no new ground.[40] He examines literary proverbs, numerical sayings, autobiographical stylization, didactic poems, dialogue, fable and allegory, didactic narrative, and prayer. Perhaps the recognition that certain themes require a particular literary medium will bear fruit. Von Rad takes great pains to emphasize the appropriateness of hymnic themes to wisdom, and to demonstrate that certain texts strike a middle position between poetry and prose.

One could even say that von Rad's ambition is to trace the movement of sages from knowledge to adoration, which he labels a small step.[41] When we realize that he follows his teacher, Alt, in claiming that Israel's wise men gathered encyclopedic lists of natural phenomena and expressed them in poetic form, we see that von Rad faces a formidable task. Alt had claimed that Solomon's unique contribution to ancient Near Eastern wisdom was the transformation of noun lists to poetry. Accordingly, exhaustive compilations of names for birds, reptiles, animals, trees, heavenly bodies, and the like achieved poetic dress only in Israel. Von Rad was particularly pleased with his discovery of such lists in Job and Ecclesiasticus, for Alt's theory now gained specific texts in its support.

This movement from knowledge to adoration did not come easily. Von Rad discusses at great length the price Israel's sages paid for this advance. They refused to locate evil outside Yahweh. As a result, believers had to come to grips with the reality of a God who was responsible for both misfortune and well-being.

The means of achieving hymnic praise comprised a virtual

emancipation of reason. To what was reason in bondage? Von Rad argues that Israel's reason was enslaved by pan sacralism, which gave way to moderate secularism, before emerging triumphantly in religious devotion. He distinguishes between old wisdom, largely secular, and theological wisdom of later vintage.

Old wisdom made considerable use of the sentence form of proverb, which registers an astute observation about life. Grounded on a conviction that an order established by the Creator in the beginning governs all reality, these sentences spoke about ways by which sages could wrest order from chaos. One could even describe them as a combined Amy Vanderbilt, Dale Carnegie, and Dear Abby course in ancient times.[42] In any event, they gave specific instructions about correct etiquette, social behavior, interpersonal relations, and whatever else was required to cope in a difficult society.

I described old wisdom as modified secularism. Von Rad insists that the fear of Yahweh belongs to early wisdom, although he concedes that this theme came to special prominence in theological wisdom. It follows that old wisdom also laid great stress upon God's unlimited power, which lies concealed with any notion of godly fear. Trust in God comprised the fundamental presupposition of all knowledge. With this claim von Rad accomplishes what few others have dared—he baptizes wisdom into Yahwism. Sages, he thinks, represent another form of Yahwism.

When von Rad moves to theological wisdom, he marvels at the similarities with other kinds of Yahwistic faith. In later wisdom, Israel's sages become worshipers. Even the literary forms they employ conform to devotional interests: hymns, didactic poems, autobiographical narrative, dispute. Furthermore, sages turn more and more to the individual and explore inner struggles and tensions requiring adequate resolution.

One must be careful lest this emphasis upon the religious pre-suppositions of sages lead to an assumption that hardly distinguishes them from prophets. Von Rad guards against such a consequence in his baptism of wisdom. He calls attention to the necessity for wisdom to prove itself, by which he means the providing of justification for every observation about life. Unlike prophets, sages could not appeal to revelation for legitimation of whatever they said. Instead, they pointed to the underlying orders of creation.[43]

In still another matter, sages parted company with prophets. While the latter achieved remarkable sophistication in interpreting history, the sages never attempted to come to grips with the writing of history. Von Rad refuses to follow his young student, Hans Jurgen Hermisson, in the hypothesis that the Yahwist and Succession Narrative show direct wisdom influence.[44] In von Rad's view, the closest the sages came to history writing was the Joseph story, which is fiction. Two things are decisive in von Rad's judgment: the Yahwist and Succession Narrative lack legitimation and recognition of life's ultimate mystery. Both features belong to the essence of wisdom.

Even Sirach does not nationalize wisdom, in spite of his inclusion of a hymn in praise of Israel's great men and women. To be sure, he draws these names from Israelite history; but his aim is more properly to religionize wisdom. Von Rad thus rejects the accuracy of Johannes Fichtner's description of Sirach as the nationalization of wisdom.[45] In my judgment, however, Fichtner's great work on Israel's wisdom, completed almost four decades earlier, offers a viable alternative to von Rad's analysis in this respect.

My reasons for this somewhat negative assessment of von Rad's interpretation of Israelite wisdom are copious, but two things stand out above all the rest. I cannot accept von Rad's major premise about the development of wisdom or his fundamental conclusion that wisdom is a branch of Yahwism. In addition, I do not think use of prophetic and narrative texts to describe special concerns of sages can be defended methodologically.[46] Von Rad errs mightily in this respect, and most of these breaches in proper procedure function to support special theories about wisdom as the mother of apocalyptic.

This brief discussion of Israel's sages has left much untouched, inasmuch as I shall take up their belief system again when considering the Old Testament world view. For now, I shall be content with an account of Israel's sages as teachers in royal courts who endeavored to expound Yahwism as they saw fit. I do wish, however, to say a few words about the fundamental theological issues to which von Rad addressed himself in *Wisdom in Israel*—the problem of general revelation.

Prior to von Rad's venture into the explication of wisdom literature, scholars generally distinguished two types of revelation, usually called general and special revelation. No one doubted the latter, if he granted the theistic hypothesis at all, but many theologians denied the presence of general revelation in the Bible. Still, allusions to a covenant with Noah implied that God grants some knowledge to all humankind, and Paul's language in Romans 1 seemed to confirm the view for Christian theologians.

Where, then, did wisdom literature fall? When we consider the further distinction between reason and revelation, the issue becomes vexing indeed. According to most scholars, wisdom literature, at least in its early stages, represents human gropings after reality in contrast to God's revealed words elsewhere in the Bible.[47] So long as the similarities between Israel's wisdom and that of Egypt and Mesopotamia occupied center stage, it was easy to consider wisdom devoid of revelation. What happens, however, when the rest of the Old Testament is shown to resemble ancient Near Eastern literature in all essentials? [48]

This is precisely the position in which modern interpreters find themselves. Faced with this barrage of parallels between Israelite and extrabiblical texts, the critic has two choices: he may abandon a belief in the special revelation of the Bible, or he may insist that we have defined that phenomenon too narrowly. Von Rad chooses the latter path.

The way had been paved for him by J. Coert Rylaarsdam, whose little book *Revelation in Jewish Wisdom Literature* [49] dealt with the tension between reason and faith with admirable perception. Von Rad threw caution to the wind, however, and exercised none of the restraint that Rylaarsdam showed. In short, von Rad hoped to prove that we have been mistaken in assuming that faith hinders knowledge. In his view, the sages believed that the person who lacked trust in God cut himself off from the secrets that an eager self-revealing Order proclaims without ceasing.

Von Rad does not ignore the decisive difference between revelation to prophets and that confronting the sages. Whereas God addresses prophets in the living present, his word to sages was spoken in the beginning, at creation. But the situation is not so simple, von Rad concedes, for God also speaks through personified wisdom in the present. In addition, the universe itself declares God's ancient message even to this very day. Thus it becomes difficult to determine where von Rad would place the sages. One thing is certain: he thinks they belong within Yahwism. In that view, he has many allies. [50]

IV. The "Historical" Portraits

As Israel's living traditions passed from "soul to soul," they aroused endless questions in the hearts of those who heard the old stories for the first time. When special rituals accompanied the telling, curiosity reached the breaking point. The solemnity of special festivals convinced the least perceptive among them that something extraordinary was taking place. An air of expectancy hovered over the congregation while those to whom Israel's religious traditions had devolved endeavored to proclaim ancient creedal affirmations.

By their very nature, traditions glance backward to an earlier age when eternity entered time and hallowed that moment. The question of origins thrust itself upon young hearts: Who was the founder of our faith? What was he like? When did he live? Where was he buried? Did he have children?

The ancient traditions pressed a claim upon everyone present. They told not only of One who entered into a special relationship with a chosen people; they also communicated God's stern demands that this holy nation become like him. Reciting the Ten

Commandments and responding to ancient self-imprecations, they asked who first received the law of God. What was this man like, who talked with the heavenly lawgiver face to face? Was he fundamentally different from these persons who listened to the strict demands with anxiety lest they prove unfaithful to God but with supreme gratitude that the Lord had revealed what pleased him?

Again and again, the now-familiar stories referred to slavery in Egypt, and to a remarkable escape from that bondage. What were the Israelites doing in foreign territory? How did they happen to fall into subjection to Pharaoh and his officials? What kept them from disappearing entirely, as the captive Israelites later did in Assyria?

On these festive occasions, one figure stood out above all the rest. Indeed, certain psalms acclaimed him a son of God. Why was the king of Judah granted special *religious* prerogatives? Who founded the monarchy in Israel? Did God give an approving nod when absolute power came to rest in the hands of a single person? What special demands has the Lord imposed upon his earthly representative?

From time to time men and women needed to get in direct touch with the One who fills heaven and earth. How was such contact possible? Who stood in the breach between heaven and earth; who mediated the word of God to ordinary citizens of ancient Israel? What was he like, this spokesman for God? Did he enjoy the vocation of prophet, or did he fight against his task with vigor?

Occasional allusions to wise men and women prompted extreme curiosity, inasmuch as these educators hardly dominated the solemn occasions. Who were the sages of Israel? What did they know that set them apart from everybody else? Did the scholars reserve secret lore for themselves, while teaching ordinary people a lesser brand of wisdom?

Such are some of the questions that surfaced in the course of Israel's religious observances. No idle curiosity, this; the questions penetrated to the very foundation of faith. But excessive interest in *human* personalities and accomplishments constituted a terrible threat. They posed the danger of crowding God out of the story. How could the human component of the drama come to fruition without detracting from the real hero of every narrative? That was the peculiar problem facing those who narrated the sacred story.

As a result of the very real danger that man might replace God as the true subject of Israel's traditions, those who phrased the tales took special pains to emphasize human frailty. Clearly, these men did not offer some sort of example that everyone was supposed to follow. At the same time, they did function paradigmatically—they pointed beyond themselves to a reality that presented itself to one and all. That reality was the living God, who gathered up the broken pieces resulting from human frailty, and fashioned from them a glorious work.

To answer Israel's anxious questions, guardians of the tradition employed their talents in a grand enterprise—the creation of portraits that would hang in Jerusalem's art gallery. In time they succeeded in portraying the father of the faith, the lawgiver, the sustainer of God's people in bondage, the king *par excellence*, the prophetic spokesman for God and the people, the scholar. Towering majestically over all these portraits, like Rembrandt's *Night Watch*, the majestic figure of Moses summoned all viewers to a choice between life and death, good and evil.

Von Rad walked through Israel's historical art gallery with lowered head, but saw far more than most critics seem to have envisioned. We turn now to his valiant attempt to recreate those vanished paintings for a people whose taste in art differs radically from that of ancient Israel.

MOSES—GOD'S LONELY SERVANT

Israel's portrait of Moses [1] was not completed in a single sitting, nor did a single artist create the masterpiece. Many artists worked on the painting, each with different brushes, colors, and techniques. Nor were these artists contemporaries; they lived at different times and in various places. Accordingly, their interests reflected those of the age in which they lived. In all likelihood, most flourished long after authentic memory of the man Moses had faded.

It follows that modern historians cannot recover the historical figure with any degree of accuracy. [2] Von Rad seems undisturbed by the fact that the real Moses lies hidden from our view, for he believes Israel's traditions have preserved what counts for something in the community of faith. Whereas the stories about Moses tell us little if anything about the historical Moses, they reveal a wealth of information about Israel's beliefs. This reality alone, von Rad thinks, matters ultimately.

The strong impulse to guard against human usurpation of the divine role fashioned many episodes in the story of Moses. Whatever else he may have been, Moses was a man. Simply that —a man with his share of human flaws. Von Rad illustrates this conviction by pointing to three events in the biblical account.

The first occurred in Egypt, that is, before the Lord had set him apart and commissioned the shepherd to lead a people out of bondage. Seeing an Egyptian brutally mistreating a fellow Hebrew, Moses sprang to the poor fellow's defense and smote the villain. In brief, the man Moses was a murderer who was forced to flee for his life.

The second incident took place after God had placed his hand upon Moses and revealed his very nature as present Lord. After spending forty days and nights on the sacred mountain with God, Moses came down to an awful discovery. Aaron and the people had reverted to paganism, and danced around a golden bull in celebration of the powers of fertility. Furious over what he saw, Moses hurled the newly granted tablets upon the ground and broke them.

This human quality knew no bounds. It led Moses to attempt the inconceivable: he talked back to God. Convinced that God had not demonstrated his presence sufficiently during the long wilderness wandering, when all the people complained bitterly and longed for the fleshpots of Egypt, Moses was imbued with some of their spirit. Von Rad was so touched by this human element in Moses that he wrote:

> In consequence, Moses, as he is presented to us, rises to gigantic stature; he surpasses the limits of ordinary human capacity; he stands as a colossus high above all the sons of men. And yet for all that, here is the true and genuine figure of a man, a figure that has power to move us by its very humanity.[3]

Von Rad observes that this man Moses possessed modesty and generosity. His long stay in divine presence changed his countenance, but he was wholly unaware that his face shone with remarkable brilliance. And when "crumbs from Moses' table" fell to seventy elders, they prophesied with abandon. Those jealous to preserve Moses' authority succeeded only in evoking from him a wish that all God's people were prophets.

But Moses was more than a man. He was a man of God, or God's servant. Von Rad asks what kind of man could stand up under the weight of God's spirit when a mere portion of it drove seventy elders to uncontrolled conduct? As God's mediator, Moses stood between an angry God and a vulnerable people, and ultimately died for them. Occupying the dangerous middle position, he walked alone into the tent of meeting. All the people stood afar off, and "followed him with their eyes." [4] Similarly, he ascended the fiery mountain alone, for none of the people dared risk talking with God.

Such special favor in God's sight seemed inviting to certain rebels, who opposed Moses before the people. Moses' own brother and sister drank this poison as well. In each instance Moses awaited God's response, for in a sense the attack centered upon Him. Finally, Moses received a reward for his suffering: although unable to enter the Promised Land, he saw from afar the fulfillment of God's promise. Von Rad remarks that this gift was far better than hope, which contains an element of uncertainty. As God spread the panorama of saving history before Moses' very eyes, God's humble servant kept his thoughts to himself.

"And so Moses died, lonely in his death as he had always been in his life (Deut. 34)." [5] God then buried his servant, von Rad writes, and by that means ruled out any possibility that the people might worship Moses and make pilgrimages to his grave site.

What brought about the significant change in the man Moses, turning him from a fleeing criminal to a dauntless leader of God's people? Von Rad discovers the explanation for this shift in Moses' call, which tells readers far more about the Lord than about the shepherd of Midian. Central to this narrative is the revelation of the divine name, a disclosure that concealed the real mystery while at the same time communicating a promise of God's presence in time of need.

In all circumstances the fundamental human query concerns the disposition of the gods: are they for us or against us? In von Rad's eyes, that question lies at the heart of Moses' inquiry about God's name. In the ancient world, professional magicians sprang up because of the desire to lay violent hands on divine powers for human ends. The key to controlling the gods rested in knowledge of their names; possessing that, men and women could summon divine assistance at will.

In such a circumstance, where knowledge of a god's secret name constituted instant power, God resolutely refused to release his name. The well-known "I am that I am" really means "I shall be present to you." Here, as in other cases of similar encounter, God refused to relinquish his name to a greedy human being. Von Rad compares the story of the angel's appearance to Manoah, who pressed for his name, and the account of Jacob's encounter with a powerful antagonist at the Jabbok river. In both instances, he argues, men sought control over the deity, and had to be satisfied with God's blessing.

The emphasis upon God's name surfaces again in the story of Moses, this time disguised under the word *glory*. Eager to behold God's glory, Moses requests the privilege of looking upon the Holy One. Now God shelters Moses with his hand while he passes by, permitting the human leader to catch a glimpse of God's back. Von Rad astutely observes that in the Old Testament men and women are permitted only to behold the completed divine work. To illustrate, he points to the story about God the surgeon who puts Adam to sleep before creating woman, and the old account of a covenant ratification when God passed between pieces of sacrificial victims while Abraham slept (Gen. 15). In reality, von Rad claims, we can only discern the footprints where God has been.

The biblical view that God strove to make known his name filled with grace, while at the same time retaining its mystery, resulted in a paradox. The gracious name enticed humans, now perched on the edge of a dangerous precipice, to seize that name for selfish purposes. In this struggle God retained full control; in short, the Lord remained free. In the end, von Rad writes, God withdrew his name from human eyes.

When one thinks of Moses, the first thing that comes to mind is the law. Tradition viewed him as the recipient of the Decalogue, the ten special commandments that came to occupy an important position in the lives of both Israel and the church. Von Rad believes ancient Israelites recited the Ten Words during the annual Feast of Tabernacles. The first two commandments merit special discussion. The initial statute calls for a separation from demons and magic, a battle that Israel waged against Canaanites with particular vigor. Von Rad emphasizes the exclusiveness of the Lord, who insists that a little bit of nature and a little bit of God will not do. Both Joshua and Elijah pose proper questions and demand a choice: how long will you maintain divided loyalties? Choose now whom you intend to serve.

The second commandment embraces material images as well as mental ones. Von Rad notes that the people did not really worship the bull that Aaron fabricated for them in an hour of need; instead, they paid homage to the power of fertility. As Hosea so powerfully demonstrates, Israel's fascination with the mystery of sex threatened to transform Yahwism into just another nature religion. By refusing to permit a resort to images, God declared that he alone would determine how revelation would take place.

A noteworthy feature of these statutes, their first and second person form, emphasizes the personal relationship presupposed. Behind the form of the commandments rests an I-Thou encounter. Furthermore, the statutes proceed to call attention to God's concern for the oppressed in the land. God's will covers the whole of life.

The absolute, categorical form of the Decalogue characterizes still other small groups of laws in the Old Testament. Von Rad refers to an old list of curses in Deuteronomy 27, which search out the hidden nooks and crannies of human lives and submit them to the judgment of an all-seeing God. Israel's law thus invades the twilight zone of human relations, covering acts performed in the privacy of one's bedroom and comparable situations.

Besides these laws which appear in the form of an absolute demand, Israel also had her share of conditional laws. Von Rad's teacher, Albrecht Alt, made a thorough study of Israelite law [6] and concluded that the normal form in which laws appeared in the ancient Near East was conditional (If an ox gores a man and he dies, then . . .). Alt believed the absolute laws were unique to Israel. He called these latter statutes apodictic, the former casuistic. This essay gained wide acceptance, although more recent research has denied the uniqueness of apodictic law.[7]

Von Rad followed his teacher in viewing case law as largely Canaanite in origin. It arose when Israel encountered new circumstances in Canaan for which their old life style had devised no system of control. In his valuable little book *Hebrew Man,*[8] the great lexicographer Ludwig Koehler wrote a significant essay in which he described justice in the gates. Von Rad accepted Koehler's account of the way elders arrived at decisions at the gate of the city, and claimed that conditional laws arose in this setting. He insisted that modern scholars must distinguish between the actual origin of these laws and their literary composition, which came much later.

The fact that case laws arose in the normal course of human decision-making did not mean that they were man-made laws. On the contrary, Israel believed these laws, too, came from God. Therefore both absolute law and conditional law were thought to have been mediated by Moses.

Who was responsible for preserving divine law? Von Rad attributes this responsibility to priests, who not only offered sacrifice but also instructed the people in God's will as made

known through his law. Indeed, the very word *torah*, which
referred to the sum total of God's law, derives from a Hebrew
word that means "to throw," hence, to instruct. As it were,
teachers throw out valuable insights for students waiting eagerly
to catch them. These guardians of the law and interpreters of
its rich meaning achieved a remarkable summary of that divine
claim upon human lives: "You shall be holy; for I the Lord
your God am holy" (Lev. 19:2).

God's law for his people was dynamic, changing with the
times. Von Rad illustrates the vitality of Israelite law in connection with beliefs about the land as God's special possession. Inasmuch as God owned the land, human occupants merely resided
on it as tenants. To remind them of this important fact, Israel
allowed the land to lie fallow every seventh year. Now when
property could no longer be measured in terms of land, sheep
and goats, but money had become the medium of exchange, laws
arose that extended the idea of divine possession of property
to money as well. Accordingly, debts were erased every seventh
year.

In some circles it is thought that Israel understood her law as
a heavy burden; this belief certainly characterizes the attacks
upon the law by the Apostle Paul. But such an understanding of
divine law contradicts everything the Old Testament says about
torah. The psalmists express profound gratitude for God's law,
which is to them a light to guide their steps and life itself.

The verbal portrait of Israel's great lawgiver hangs in a
gallery, and thus must be viewed in a larger context. Von Rad
insists that we understand Moses correctly only if we see him in
his role in the Hexateuch. The theme of this literary complex of
Genesis through Joshua is promise and fulfillment. The larger
work covers an amazing time period: from creation to the occupation of the promised land by the people of God.

Perhaps as no one before, von Rad perceives the significance

of Genesis 12:1–3 in this narrative. This text functions as a
transition in God's manner of dealing with the human race.
Divine activity narrows to a single family, Abraham and his
descendants. But the peculiar task of this chosen people accomplishes a widening of God's blessing to incorporate the
whole world. Through Abraham, all peoples of the earth will
be blessed; von Rad refuses to interpret this much disputed text
as a reference to oath-taking in Abraham's name.[9] Instead, he
insists that in Abraham God's saving activity sweeps all mankind
into its wondrous path.

The promise of a blessing, like the land, and indeed all God's
gifts to his people, is precisely that—a gift. Von Rad uses a
graphic phrase to describe Israel's total dependence upon God.
In discussing the story about manna which God provided in the
wilderness, he remarks that we live from hand to mouth in all
our dealings with God. In truth, we cannot write a check on God
without having it bounce; our morality places no claim upon
Israel's Lord, who freely gives his bounty.

In a sense, this was precisely the issue under discussion while
Israel was poised to enter the promised land. An enemy king,
Balak, summons a man skilled in magic and urges him to curse
Israel. This magician, Balaam, enacts a drama with the fate of
God's people hanging in the balance, and they are totally unaware of the danger facing them. In this old story, von Rad
observes, God lets human beings act, but proceeds to nullify
the effects of their action. In this way God guides the course
of human history. In the process, he rendered magic powerless.
Balaam who came to curse, stayed to bless. This old seer beheld
a marvelous sight, the coming of the Messiah, von Rad contends.
From this narrative it follows that all history has an inner
meaning that is grasped only by the ones upon whom God lays
his hand.

All history has a secret inner side, which is hidden from the eyes of the natural man. The story of Balaam turns history inside out and makes the miracle plain.[10]

What, then, was the revelation that came to Moses, and through him, to God's people? Von Rad sums up that message as follows: (1) a calling of a people chosen by God to live directly under his guidance and obedient to his will; (2) a calling to pilgrimage; (3) a revelation of God who dwells in the midst of his people in judgment and mercy; (4) the communication of a law, Israel's guardian and guide, which was accepted and observed joyously; and (5) a vision of an expanding purpose to be fulfilled when all nations are brought into God's kingdom.

Von Rad does not stop here. Indeed, as a confessing Christian, he seems compelled to say more.[11] In the events surrounding Moses he sees types of things that seem to appear in all their fullness in Jesus as Christ. We could multiply examples, but two suffice to illustrate the point. Israel's insistence upon the importance of the land has something to say about the absolute necessity of affirming that Jesus died at Golgotha. The Christ event was no myth, von Rad insists, for Jesus really gave his life in behalf of human sins. Furthermore, only a people schooled in the first two commandments could arrive at the belief that Jesus the Christ was wrought by God and God alone. The second example concerns Moses' role as suffering servant. Von Rad writes that Moses pointed to Jesus in his lonely life and death for God's people. What was shown dimly in Moses, he believes, has come with clarity in Jesus.

ABRAHAM—GOD'S VICTIM

Beside this majestic portrait of Moses hangs another picture of one who tasted the bitter gall of loneliness. This dark painting portrays the father of the faith, Abraham of old. Whereas Moses was cut off from human companions, but basked in God's smile, Abraham walked upon a mountain into God-forsakenness, comforted only by his beloved son whom he intended to sacrifice at God's command. The lonely servant Moses had God's friendship; Abraham was not so sure on that score.

Indeed, a strong case could be made for viewing Abraham as God's fool. Obedient to divine summons, Abraham forsook father and mother, turned his back upon his country, and ventured forth into an unknown future. All this he did, fully confident that God would be true to his threefold promise of land, progeny, and blessing. Upon arriving at the land that God showed him, it seemed that Abraham was the victim of a cruel joke. The land promised him was already occupied, and besides, a famine had spread throughout the country. In his whole lifetime Abraham never possessed the land. To be sure, he built an altar at Shechem, and spread the aroma of his faith (Calvin); but the most Abraham ever owned was a cave in which he buried his wife. In the land of promise he walked amid pagans, an interloper and inferior.

The promise of innumerable children and grandchildren also seemed like a jest, particularly when Sarah passed the age of bearing. Small wonder she burst forth in laughter when some visitors told her husband that she would bear a child in her old age.

Egypt's Pharaoh and Abimelech king of Gerar found sufficient cause to question the truth of the promise that all peoples would be blessed by Abraham. On the contrary, Abraham's careless handling of the truth and concern only for his own wellbeing jeopardized the lives of these rulers and placed them and Sarah in compromising situations. With good reason, then, von Rad asks if Abraham was not obliged to wonder whether the divine promise was a cruel joke.

If such a question arises from the delayed fulfillment of God's promises, how much more it accosts anyone who struggles to understand the story of Abraham's sacrifice,[12] to use the subjective genitive preferred by von Rad. Confronted by such a story about God's monstrous test of his faithful servant, even men and women of faith must quake—and wonder if they too are fools.

How, then, should one read such a story? Von Rad furnishes some important clues to a proper reading of Genesis 22. First, and foremost, the reader must be open to the terror filling the account. We dare not let our desire to protect innocent children from frightening stories rob us of the necessity to come to grips with this text. Nor ought we shy away from it because of the foreign nature of the story. Worse than that, however, is the tendency to disbelieve the account, and thus to divest it of its remarkable power. Our greatest enemy, it follows, is a readiness to trust God in any and every circumstance, which prevents us from hearing what this story wishes to say.

Second, we must rely upon the richness of our own experience of reality if we hope to plumb the depths of this story. That is, the reader must prepare for a dialogue with the text, knowing that we are what dialogue with God makes of us. This means that our success in understanding the story about Abraham's offering of his son stands in exact proportion to the depth dimension of our own encounters with God.

A third clue resides in the larger context within which the story appears, a hint provided by the text itself in Genesis 22:15–18, which renews God's original promises. Links with the previous narrative occur throughout the story itself, both in language and theme. Although von Rad perceived some of these connections, he missed the most striking one, in my judgment. As I see it, Genesis 12:1–3 stands over against Genesis 22:1–19. In the former a son sacrifices his father, in the latter a father offers up his son.[13] If in truth salvation history begins at Genesis 12:1–3, it very nearly ends at Genesis 22:1–19.

At one time this dreadful story of human sacrifice functioned as a cultic aetiology; it demonstrated the legitimacy of substituting animal sacrifices for humans. Von Rad refuses to concede this functional meaning to the current narrative. Instead, he insists that such a purpose had disappeared long before. The aim of this tale, von Rad believes, is to answer a fundamental question: what does it mean to fear God?

A proper interpretation of the text under consideration takes note of an awful silence that thunders in the night. Erich Auerbach's perceptive analysis of Hebrew narrative over against Greek epic [14] provides von Rad with a significant stance from which to view the dialogue within the biblical story. Auerbach observed that Homeric narrative art leaves little to the imagination, but supplies abundant detail, while Hebraic stories seem "fraught with background." The biblical narrator left much to the imagination, satisfied that the listener would fill in the rest. Economy of language characterizes the entire story; this brevity stands out impressively in the brief dialogues that fill the narrative.

Von Rad rejected the usual view that Abraham knew that everything would turn out well in the end. "My son, God will provide . . ." was neither a lie to silence an inquisitive boy nor Abraham's assurance that everything was under control. No, Abraham spoke more than he understood, uttered truth that he did not fully grasp.

In truth, divine silence would have been preferable to the monstrous demand imposed upon a loving father. Von Rad faces this bitter truth as fully as any other critic, in my judgment. Israel's long history knew moments of testing, when God seemed bent on destroying the very people he loved. This story declares that at times God seems to be his own worst enemy, but Israel need not worry overmuch.

When dialogue rarely occurs in a story, we expect the few instances of speech to utter something profound. How disappointing, therefore, must be Abraham's conversation with Isaac. The two discuss ordinary concerns: fire, wood, sacrificial victim. The narrator does not use this powerful moment, set off by the most ominous refrain in the Bible ("Now the two of them walked together") to present the key to understanding the terrible story.

Nor does Abraham relieve the oppressive silence marking the climax of the story. We expect a word of gratitude because God changed his mind in the nick of time, but we are disappointed. In silent obedience, Abraham accepts the command to offer up his son. The ordeal past, he returns alone to Sarah without a word on his lips—a silence Jewish tradition found too grievous to bear.[15] Von Rad writes that this silence, which speaks eloquently, threatens to become the real mystery of the story. Unlike Job, Abraham does not dispute God's right to do with him as he pleased. In short, neither gratitude nor dispute shattered the silence that embraced Abraham in this dark hour.

Abraham's silence arose from an awareness that no word, however profound, suffices in such a time as this. Indeed, the story only heightens life's enigmas. Von Rad sees Abraham's dilemma with exceptional clarity: perform the sacrifice, and the lights go out; refuse, and God departs from him. Isaac is no ordinary son; he represents God's promise to Abraham. Having turned his back upon the past, Abraham now must abandon his only prospects for a future. To Abraham, as to almost all Old Testament figures, death introduced the silence of eternity.

Abraham's three-day trek constituted a march into God-

forsakenness. For Isaac, it was a journey into oblivion.[16] Von
Rad writes that God led Abraham to Golgotha! Others experienced the darkness of divine withdrawal: the psalmists who
lamented their awful state; Job; the prophets. From these unfortunate people, and yet most fortunate, Israel learned an
important lesson. The God who enters human lives freely withdraws from their midst; *deus revelatus* becomes *deus ab-
sconditus*.[17]

Although Abraham walked into God-forsakenness, he discovered an amazing fact. God accompanied him all the time.
Von Rad thus qualifies his claim that Abraham experienced
divine abandonment. Rather than attempting to explain this
paradox, we should recognize that the story alerts the believer
to the real possibility that he or she will sooner or later come
face to face with life's contradictions. Precisely at this point,
von Rad observes, this story takes up a favorite topic of Israel's
wisdom literature. As proof that God continued to walk with
him through the dark hour, Abraham experiences renewed
blessing, certainly no sign of one who has been abandoned by
God.

How do we react to such a story as this? We cannot remain
neutral, however much we try. Von Rad gathers together representative samples of various responses to this narrative: Martin
Luther's comments on the chapter; Sören Kierkegaard's lyrical
panegyric; some caustic observations by a Marxist philosopher,
Leszek Kolakowski; Rembrandt's repeated attempts to capture
the decisive moment and preserve it forever on canvas.[18]

Confronted with such a story, we protest vigorously, both in
the name of humanity and in behalf of God as we understand
him. Von Rad writes that the text succeeds in shattering our
sacred images of God. It functions iconoclastically, breaking
into tiny pieces our most cherished convictions about God. The
disturbing story of a monstrous test imposed by God upon a

faithful servant warns us that God will not permit himself to be enslaved, even in human minds. When least expected, he strikes out in new directions and exercises sovereign freedom.

Whatever else this story communicates, it proclaims one message above all else; we walk in the midst of profound mystery, which encircles us like the air we breathe. It is fitting that the father of the faith lifted up his eyes in time to catch a glimpse of the fateful mountain, for Moriah and Golgotha confront Jews and Christians as the supreme mystery of faith. Von Rad insists that the author of this story, whom scholars call the Elohist, knew that *God* put Israel to the test again and again. For him there was nothing dark *outside God.*

We must resist the temptation to view Abraham's silence as stoic obedience. To be sure, he moves about his task like a sleepwalker, but the story suggests that powerful emotions overwhelmed him. Von Rad repeats an astute observation of Hermann Gunkel's, that Abraham carried the dangerous implements (knife, fire) lest the lad Isaac harm himself.[19] Furthermore, Abraham rises early in the morning, so eager is he to carry out God's command. Rembrandt perceived the competing impulses within Abraham's breast more fully than anyone else, it seems, for he sought to depict Abraham as both reluctant and eager to sacrifice his beloved son. Love of God and love of son wage a mighty battle in Abraham's soul.

We have described this story as Abraham's. One could approach it from Isaac's standpoint, for it was his story, too. Von Rad remarks that this narrative differs from the account of Jephthah's sacrifice of his only daughter. Here the father communicates his intentions, and his daughter willingly acquiesces. Not a word is spoken to Isaac in warning, nor do we learn of the effect upon him in the end. Instead, we have a perplexing separation of father and son after the incident. Abraham returns to his servants, and subsequently to Beersheba, *alone.*[20] For

what happened to Isaac, we must search Jewish tradition. As
Shalom Spiegel has demonstrated so ably,[21] that search con-
firms the remarkable success of this story in forcing later believers to acknowledge divine mystery.

JOSEPH—GOD'S ALIEN WORK

A third portrait in Israel's gallery of art depicted Joseph
in Egypt.[22] The title of this painting was "God's alien work."
In this picture of one who knows how to speak wisely and
when to be silent, von Rad perceives a model for Israel's young
men within the wisdom schools. In a word, Joseph was a manifestation of the wisdom ideal of an educated person.

How does von Rad reach this extraordinary conclusion?
He first isolates the Joseph story from its context in Genesis.
Whereas the other narratives of that book consist of originally
independent incidents covering twenty to thirty verses, the
Joseph novella extends to nearly four hundred verses. As far
as length is concerned, then, the story of Joseph differs significantly from the patriarchal narratives. Furthermore, the
content of the two bodies of literature differs markedly. The
Joseph story contains no historicopolitical interests, and lacks,
in von Rad's view, cultic-aetiological concerns entirely.

The Joseph narrative also bears a distinctive literary style:
the depiction of involved psychological situations, and the use
of telling phrases. In this regard von Rad likens the story of
Joseph to the Court History of David (2 Sam. 6 through
1 Kings 2). Gunkel's passing remark that the author of the
Joseph narrative delighted in all things foreign struck von Rad
as essentially correct. This fascination with the exotic includes
an enlightened interest in the customs of Egypt, the magnifi-
cence of the court, the installation of a vizier, storage of crops,
and mummification.

The decisive clue for von Rad resides in the anthropological character of the Joseph story, "a concentration upon the phenomenon of man in the broadest sense, his potentialities and his limitations, his psychological complexity and profundity." [23] Von Rad mentions, among other things, the distress of the soul (42:21), dumb astonishment (45:3, 26), mutual looks of fear (42:28), agitations of conscience (43:18), seething emotion (43:30). In accord with this focus upon everything human, the Joseph story does not tell of God's appearing, speaking, acting, and so forth. On the contrary, the narrator speaks of God only indirectly (with two exceptions). Even Joseph's dreams retain an element of ambiguity. To be sure, their ultimate source is God, but the way they are described leaves open the possibility of viewing them as vainglorious desire on the part of a spoiled, pampered young son.

The patriarchal narratives display no interest in the "Gestalt" of Abraham, Isaac or Jacob, von Rad contends. The nearest they come to such an interest occurs in the story of Abraham's near sacrifice of Isaac, and this episode constitutes an exception. How differently things are perceived in the Joseph novella, where all eyes focus upon the figure of Joseph, whose entire life span is treated. "To be sure, every story is shaped by the special spirit of its narrator, and every storyteller is influenced in return by the intellectual atmosphere in which he lives." [24] Believing this firmly, von Rad searches for the age that gave voice to such emphases.

His attention comes to rest on the Solomonic era, which von Rad viewed as a veritable enlightenment. Prior to this intellectual revolution, God's action was bound to institutions such as holy war, charisma of chosen persons, miracle, cult. In Solomon's day the ancient sacral traditions had died, and God's action had changed radically. Now the human heart becomes the principal realm for God's providential and judging activity.

Now if the Joseph story manifests the spirit of the Solomonic enlightenment, what function did it perform within that setting? Von Rad argues that the twin virtues of an educated man (outspokenness and sound counsel) had to be cultivated. For that purpose a model was necessary, a guiding pattern for those who aspired to nobility of character. Believing that the early sentence literature in Proverbs belongs to the setting of the royal court, von Rad turns to this source for confirmation of his thesis that Joseph depicts an ideal sage.

In this analysis of ancient proverbs, three things stand out above all the rest: the foundation of all knowledge, limits to knowledge, and discipline. Von Rad recognizes the significance of the concept of godly fear in the thought of the wise (Prov. 1:7; 15:33; cf. Gen. 42:18). Thus wisdom works outwardly from the cult and divine revelation, he claims, and not towards them. This feature accounts for the undogmatic and realistic impression left by the sentence literature. Still, such an approach to reality surrenders to absolute standards of divine law, as we see in Joseph's refusal to commit adultery with Potiphar's eager wife. This incident calls to mind the frequent warnings within Proverbs against the strange or foreign woman.

Second, the sentence literature concedes ultimate ignorance in the face of life's imponderables. "A man's mind plans his way, but Yahweh directs his steps" (Prov. 16:9); "Many are the plans in the mind of man, but it is Yahweh's purpose that will be established" (Prov. 19:21). Von Rad asks whether Joseph's comment that his brothers meant evil against him but God meant it for good (Gen. 50:20) is not a wisdom saying that has been adapted for the story.

The immediate danger of such stress upon God's hiddenness finds expression in Proverbs 20:24: "A man's steps are ordered by Yahweh; how then can man understand his way?" As long as an inspired interpreter exists, such emphasis is salutary.

Lacking one, skepticism takes hold and eventually prevails. Even within the Joseph story, von Rad detects an element of resignation, the underside of the sage's buoyant confidence. Once a deep cleavage arises between divine and human purposes, human activity becomes so heavily fettered by divine control that it comes perilously close to losing significance (Prov. 21:30–31; Amenemope 19:14). Von Rad nods in the direction of Ecclesiastes,[25] which sinks its roots deeply into the skepticism of the Joseph narrative and sentence wisdom.

Israel's sages realized that the educational ideal demanded conscious effort on the part of those who hoped to achieve it. Self-control had to be learned, often in the "school of hard knocks." Thus we hear again and again of the positive role discipline plays in education. Anyone who wished to succeed in administrative circles needed to master his tongue; this accomplishment includes both the negative dimension of learning when to be silent and the positive art of public speaking (Prov. 22:29; Ecclus. 8:8; Ptahhotep 24). Von Rad writes that Joseph restrains his lips (cf. Prov. 10:19), conceals knowledge (cf. Prov. 12:23), and above all controls his passions. In his case, discipline came in the midst of adversity. Although he has every reason to cherish revenge on his brothers, Joseph magnanimously foregoes retribution, refusing to be in the place of God toward his brothers. Von Rad observes that the "writer intends us to be amazed at the extraordinary control which Joseph is able to exercise over his emotions."[26] One must remember that such suppression of emotion ran counter to everything we know about the Hebraic instinct.

We spoke above of the narrator's indirect manner of speaking about God, with two exceptions. Von Rad makes much of these two examples of "concentrated theology" within the Joseph story. The first theological statement occurs in the recognition scene (Gen. 45:5–8), where Joseph contrasted his brothers'

actions with those of God. Whereas they sold Joseph, God kept
him alive to preserve life. This leads von Rad to write: "God has
all the threads firmly in his hands even when men are least
aware of it." [27] The image illustrates the danger residing within
such theology: human beings are not puppets. Hence a po-
tentially comforting notion carries in its wake a heavy burden,
the suspicion that human actions and decisions count for naught.

The second direct theological statement contrasts the brothers'
intentions with God's, and suggests that God can use evil to
accomplish good (Gen. 50:20). In Joseph's view, God's hand
leads through human guilt and all kinds of trouble, eventually
arriving at a gracious goal. Although we might be tempted to
view Joseph's cat-and-mouse treatment of his brothers as cruel,
von Rad argues that he merely put them to two tests in order to
determine whether they have truly changed or not. Thus we see
how forgiveness among men reaches deeply into the relationship
between man and God. In this matter, as in all others, von Rad
concludes that Joseph was a modern man in his day.[28]

DAVID—GOD'S SINNER

The fourth portrait that seemed worthy of von Rad's special
attention was that of King David,[29] the man after God's own
heart. Here we encounter one whose whole life was a mass of
contradictions, a father whose blind devotion to his sons almost
brought his "throne and empire to the brink of catastrophe," [30]
and whose libidinous extravagance very nearly swept the royal
family to ruin.

What do we know about the youthful David? Precious little,
it seems. Three mutually contradictory accounts endeavor to
explain his appearance at Saul's court. In one, the least reliable, in von Rad's judgment, Yahweh calls David and sets

him apart for future greatness. An appropriate prophet, the renowned Samuel, communicates this special favor to the humble son of Jesse. Another version focuses upon Saul's madness as the occasion for bringing David, a skillful harpist, to the royal court. In this account, David's music soothed the mind of a demented king. Naturally, such a gifted musician must have composed psalms, later liturgists believed. Thus they credited David with a considerable repertoire of songs. The third view of David's arrival at the royal court celebrates his remarkable skill as a fighter. In this version, the youngster volunteers to meet the fearsome Goliath in single combat, and emerges from the skirmish as the victor.

In a number of stories David stands over against Israel's first king in a struggle for survival. In von Rad's view, David is the real subject of these episodes, and Saul's tragic fate grows out of a loss of charisma. We shall forego analysis of these narratives in order to concentrate on the Court History, which rivals Deuteronomy in importance for von Rad's understanding of the Old Testament.

We turn first to the scope of the narrative that von Rad views as the beginning of historical writing in ancient Israel. In a significant departure from the customary explanation of the reference to Michal's barrenness in 2 Samuel 6:16, 20–23 as a tailpiece for the story about an endangered ark, Leonhard Rost understood the text as the real starting point of the Succession Narrative.[31] Von Rad accepted Rost's discovery of the actual theme of this story—who will reign on the throne of David?—and reinforced that thesis by a brilliant analysis.

He first makes some observations about the nature of history writing, claiming that only Israel and Greece wrote history in the ancient world. The Hebrews possessed three predisposing features that gave birth to historiography: a historical sense, an

outstanding talent for narrative presentation, and a tendency to
see God at work in all events, even those usually attributed to
demons. Von Rad writes:

> Israel owes to its unique religious faith a capacity to see and
> understand as history what is really no more than a succession of
> isolated occurrences. . . . The Israelites came to a historical
> way of thinking, and then to history writing, by way of their
> belief in the sovereignty of God in history.[32]

The first stage of history writing consisted of hero sagas.[33]
In one respect, these sagas differ markedly from genuine history: they remove the action from human hands. In truth, God
is the real subject of the hero saga, von Rad remarks. Another
difference between hero saga and genuine history concerns the
nature of the individual episodes making up the story. In saga,
as, for example, the Gideon narrative, the incidents are independent tales, chiefly cultic or aetiological.

The Court History advances a step beyond the hero saga, and
in doing so introduces genuine history into the ancient world.
Von Rad comments on the matchless style, lucidity, and restraint typifying this intimate disclosure of fatal illness within
the royal household. The mood is set at the outset: a queen's
scorn for her husband eventuates in her sterility. Gloom settles
over the Davidic household. Coming immediately after this
unsettling bit of news, Nathan's wonderful prophecy promising
that God would build a dynasty for David serves to heighten
the suspense. How can that be, since Michal is barren? Will
Yahweh keep his promise?

That question presses itself upon the reader with particular
force once David's sexual appetite invades the sanctity of another's marriage. In this instance, adultery leads to murder as
a means of covering up the king's nefarious deed and removing

any opposition to love. Must Yahweh rescind his promise now that David has demonstrated his true character? Von Rad observes that this incident functions to introduce the one who will eventually give birth to David's successor.

David's libidinous conduct not only paved the way for the resolution of the problem described above as the theme of the story. It also set into motion forces that soon destroyed the integrity of his family. Amnon, the heir apparent, repeats his father's folly, and this time the victim belongs to the royal household. Tamar's nobility of birth explodes in her plea with her brother: "No, my brother, such a thing is not done in Israel." At length another son also insults his father *publicly* by sexual behavior that recalls David's rooftop indiscretion. Von Rad takes note of the "air of austere nobility" that "broods over the whole work" despite the subject matter.[34] The stories are reported with delicacy and uncommon restraint, without the slightest touch of gossip.

David's awful sin threatens to abort God's plan for building a dynasty. Someone must pay for the twin offenses of adultery and murder. The story of that payment throws light on another feature of David's complex personality: his strong independent spirit. Contrary to common custom, David refused to mourn the death of his child of lust. So long as the child lived, David pleaded with God that the baby be spared; once death occurred, the grieving father arose and resumed his daily routine. The time had passed, he reasoned, for altering the child's fate. That death, it should be noted, was a special sign that God had forgiven David.

An indulgent father who could not hold his son's affections proved capable of sustaining loyalty from foreigners in his service. Von Rad highlights the scenes in which the Philistine Ittai and the aged Barzillai demonstrate their loyalty. The hasty retreat from Jerusalem on the occasion of Absalom's rebellion, together with David's return journey after that revolt had been suppressed, has taken on the trappings of a penitential march and triumphal return. The contrast between the two Davids can hardly be sharper. En route, he suffers incredible humiliation relieved only by Ittai's faithfulness—and the prospect that the counselor Hushai just conceivably could frustrate Ahithophel's counsel, with God's help. Returning, David bestows kingly forgiveness upon his foes. Now "the noble behavior of the King, purified as he is by his suffering, shines like brilliant light on all around him." [35]

The key to the entire story resides in the episode that is often taken to belong to the story of Solomon (1 Kings 1). Here the narrator brings into the open for the first time the central question that has occupied his thinking all along: who will sit upon the throne of David? The story of the youthful Abishag's fruitless efforts to revive the aged David's sexual powers dramatically poses the problem, at least to ancient readers. An impotent king is no king at all. Von Rad draws the necessary conclusion from this story: the successor to David must come from the surviving sons, for there will be no more. It follows that the story ends when Solomon secures the throne.

So far we have carefully avoided any reference to what von Rad believes is the crowning achievement of this powerful story: the restraint with which it speaks of God. In his view, three theological statements transform the narrative, turning ordinary events into saving history. The first of these pronounces judgment upon David for his adulterous act (2 Sam. 11:27); the second anticipates the resolution of the problem about David's successor (2 Sam. 12:24) by reporting that Yahweh loved Solomon. The last one announces the simple truth that human counsel comes to naught unless God wills it (2 Sam. 17:14). Even Ahithophel's sound advice, which was as certain as a divine oracle, cannot withstand heavenly opposition.

The cause-and-effect pattern operates so effectively in this story that one would think even God could discover no place in which to insert his hand. Still, von Rad writes, "secretly it is he who has brought all to pass; all the threads are in his hands; his activity embraces the great political events no less than the hidden counsels of human hearts." [36]

Inasmuch as the story deals with God's anointed one, its theme is messianic. With this bold statement, von Rad endeavors to signify the centrality of the theological problem being discussed in the profane arena. The story shows that the anointed was humiliated in the deepest possible manner, and his throne fell victim to tyrannous revolt. "Why, here we find also the anointed who suffers," von Rad exclaims.[37]

In this regard we need to look elsewhere for a valuable insight into Israel's ancient concept of sacral office, i.e., 2 Samuel 24. This story reports a deliberate breach of sacred regulation on David's part, the taking of a census for military purposes, and inevitable punishment. In this situation "David did what was quite unexpected, but precisely in so doing he flung himself through the thick curtain of the divine anger directly on God's heart." [38] Von Rad notes that the Chronicler was unwilling to endure the tension within the narrative between a God who entices to an act and subsequently punishes for the deed. Instead, the Chronicler introduces Satan as tempter of David. In this, as in other ways, this later author labored to whitewash this scandalous king who was a man after God's own heart.

We have by no means captured the multifaceted personality of King David. To accomplish that task, we would need to consider the intriguing role of Joab, the *unanointed*, in securing David's kingdom; the touches of human kindness that David occasionally displayed, particularly his concern not to expose his men to shame; the moment of deepest craving for life-sustaining water; and above all, his poignant cry over his dead son: "O my son Absalom, my son, my son Absalom! Would I had died instead of you, O Absalom, my son, my son!" (2 Sam. 18:33; 19:1 in Hebrew).

JEREMIAH—GOD'S ABANDONED PROPHET

The fifth portrait that von Rad appreciated for its devastatingly human quality has twin panels. On one panel the artist has painted a self-portrait; on the other, a faithful friend has rendered his version of the subject. I refer to the prophet Jeremiah, whose personal confessions lay bare his innermost being, and about whom the scribe Baruch wrote a "biography" that approaches a *via dolorosa*, a way of sorrow.[39]

Such a painting allows us to view the prophet from vastly different perspectives. On the one hand, we see the events as an outsider, and follow Jeremiah along his path of suffering. But we lack essential data: how did he react to ridicule, calumny, and physical abuse? Fortunately, Jeremiah did not keep silent, but cried out against the heavens. This response has come down to us, perhaps because others saw something typical or representative in Jeremiah's suffering. Inasmuch as the menace hovering over Jeremiah reached beyond a single individual, von Rad suggests that the prophet came to typify the suffering nation Israel, a conclusion to which the Jewish scholar, Sheldon Blank, came independently in a recent essay.[40]

In order to grasp the full import of Jeremiah's self-portrait, we need to examine the context in which he functioned as a prophet and the traditions to which he was heir. In the first place, Jeremiah belonged to a priestly family, banished to Anathoth during Solomon's day. It should come as no surprise that the prophet renews the old mode of stating that Israel's complete failure is cultic, and that he often thinks in cultic categories. In this regard, as in others, Jeremiah walked in Hosea's footsteps.

This affinity is so striking that von Rad insists upon a connecting link between Hosea and Jeremiah. Naturally, he finds that point of contact in Hosea's hypothetical disciples with whom Jeremiah was acquainted. Von Rad contends that this association with Hosea's disciples alone explains Jeremiah's dependence upon Hosea in ideas and *word choice*.

In the second place, we note an astonishing thing when we examine the traditions that Jeremiah seems to have inherited. Nowhere does the Zion tradition, so important to Isaiah of Jerusalem, shape Jeremiah's thinking. Quite the contrary, he even calls that tradition into question with the "blasphemous" attack upon the temple (chs. 7, 26). Instead of proclaiming Yahweh's protection of Jerusalem, Jeremiah returns to the ancient traditions: exodus, conquest, covenant.

A third thing that merits some attention at this point is the decisive shift in the formal categories of prophecy that occurs in Jeremiah. With him, poetry dominates. The old literary forms begin to break up; no longer do diatribe and threat characterize prophetic speech. Instead, exhortation abounds, together with lyrical poetry. Furthermore, the distinction between God's word and the words of the prophet vanishes, and with that, the tone shifts to suffering and complaint. Description thus comes to characterize Jeremiah's speeches, which possess the ruthlessness of earlier classical prophecy. Von Rad writes that Jeremiah does not stop short of criticizing the holiest of all things.

What was this fearless prophet like? The self-portrait discloses a side of the prophet that links him with the previous figures I have discussed as belonging to Israel's art gallery. Whatever else Jeremiah knew, he experienced suffering on every hand. The confessions, according to von Rad's enumeration, consist of the following texts: 11:18–23; 12:1–6; 15:10–12, 15–21; 17:12–18; 18:18–23; 20:7–18.

Jeremiah's confessions possess a note of sadness that lingers

on and on, and in the end they take leave of Jeremiah abandoned
by his God. He now utters soliloquies; in 20:7, 9 "the God
whom the prophet addresses no longer answers him." [41] Von
Rad expresses dismay that Jeremiah did not interpret his suffering as in some sense representative. He writes: "Never for
a moment did it occur to him that this mediatorial suffering
might have a meaning in the sight of God." [42]

The confessions expose Jeremiah's shortcomings with brutal
frankness. In 15:10–18, Yahweh answers with a stern rebuke.
Here he accuses the prophet of betraying his calling. In 12:1–5,
Jeremiah concedes his case against God in the initial sentence:
"Yahweh is always in the right." Von Rad views this passage as
a discussion of a vexing problem: how is the individual's share
in Yahweh's gifts apportioned? The resolution of this issue fails
to generate hope for the prophet: "One is haunted by the impression that the darkness keeps growing, and eats more deeply
into the prophet's soul." [43]

In the end, Jeremiah hurls a bold accusation in God's face:
"You have taken advantage of my simplicity." Actually, he accuses God of seduction and rape; the choice of the same word
for seducing a young girl emphasizes Jeremiah's sense of out-
rage over God's treatment of him. It is clear that Jeremiah finds
it increasingly difficult to see where he is going, although per-
ceiving in these confessions that the final destiny will be divine
abandonment. Von Rad writes: "The external circumstance of
the order in which they appear in itself outlines a road which
leads step by step into ever greater despair." [44]

What about the external description of Jeremiah? Can we
look to Baruch's narrative account of the prophet for a positive
assessment of Jeremiah's destiny? Here, at least, we expect a
more objective description, since Baruch could stand some
distance from the storm's center and describe its progress with
considerably more objectivity.

We observe at the outset that Baruch does not tease us with stories about divine intervention in miraculous fashion. Von Rad contrasts Baruch's manner of writing to that of an earlier age, the Elijah legend, and the late story of Daniel in the lion's den. In behalf of the prophet Jeremiah, God neither sends food by ravens nor stops up a lion's mouth. In Baruch's account, nothing like that relieved the suffering of God's persecuted prophet. In truth, not a single allusion to God's guiding hand relieves the impression that in Jeremiah's agony "a human being has in a unique fashion borne a part in the divine suffering." [45]

Like his mentor, Baruch does not shy away from the truth, even when it hurts. As a consequence, he depicts Jeremiah in compromising circumstances, even for an ancient reader (Jer. 38:14–27). Here the prophet seems wholly willing to bend the truth, so fond of life is he. How vastly different is this account of a spineless figure from other stories of men who chose to die for the truth! Perhaps we should not be too hard on Jeremiah. After all, he seems completely bereft of hope: "What is particularly sad is the absence of any good or promising issue." [46]

Even if personally Jeremiah lacked hope, what promise did he offer the people themselves? Von Rad remarks that Jeremiah's hope for the future was disappointingly sober. In the well-known passage that speaks of a new covenant (31:31–34), Jeremiah comes perilously close to abdicating human freedom. Like Hosea before him, this prophet who endured God's suffering speaks about the destruction of the human will and the substitution of God's will. Convinced that only God could bring his people back to him (13:23, "Can the Ethiopian change his skin/or the leopard his spots?/Then also you can do good/who are accustomed to do evil"), Jeremiah believed that God would implant his will within the human soul.

Jeremiah's vision for the future of God's people contains a striking allusion to a ruler whom God will cause to approach

Him. (30:21). Rejecting the priestly interpretation of this
anointed one, von Rad understands the reference as something
more than the ancient belief that beholding God endangered
one's life. Much more is being said by a person who knew what
it meant to risk his life on God's behalf.

> In his view—and here again we recognize Jeremiah—the most
> important thing is that the anointed one risks his life, and in this
> way holds open access to God in the most personal terms pos-
> sible.[47]

In short, Israel's ruler will have ready access to the most secret
counsel of the sovereign Lord.

Surely, Jeremiah's *via dolorosa* prepared him to expect a
comparable role for the anointed one. One could go a step
further. The prophet Jeremiah's sense of Yahweh's overpower-
ing presence gave birth to the conviction that an alien will
would take up residence in all God's people. Certainly, Jeremiah's experience with the divine word could only be described
as invasion from without by a power that he found irresistible.
That mighty word burned like a fire within his innermost being,
and crushed him with the impact of a hammer. By choosing the
emotion-filled term *rape*, Jeremiah made it clear that he was
powerless to resist the God who fills heaven and earth, the One
who is both very near and far away. In Israel's case, that overwhelming invasion from without augured salvation, for it would
assure obedience to God's will. For Jeremiah, on the other hand,
this mighty force constituted betrayal by God.

THE CHOSEN ONE

A single theme pervades these five "historical portraits."
Moses, Abraham, Joseph, David, Jeremiah tasted the bitter

dregs of abandonment and dwelt alone in a crowd. Each experienced the pain of loneliness, the agony of suffering for others. Their experiences, taken together, leave a terrifying impression upon the reader. Is this what it means to be chosen by God? Must the servant of God walk inevitably into darkness and God forsakenness, knowing at last a silence that is stiller than that encountered by Elijah in God's cave?

V. The Tradition that
Transcends History

In his essay, "Some Aspects of the Old Testament World View," von Rad issued a remarkable warning to Old Testament scholars: "If I am right, we are nowadays in serious danger of looking at the theological problems far too much from the one-sided standpoint of an historically conditioned theology." [1] Perhaps few persons needed such a *caveat* more than von Rad himself, the "little historical monoman." What led him to this surprising position?

The answer is not difficult to discover: he had begun to study Israel's wisdom literature, which had long been ignored by theologians whose major interest was saving history. Indeed, this corpus of literature (Job, Proverbs, Ecclesiastes, Ecclesiasticus, Wisdom of Solomon, and a few Psalms) was looked upon by many as a source of embarrassment, an alien body within the canon. Try as they might, these interpreters could not apply with any degree of satisfaction standards derived from analysis of Yahwistic texts, inasmuch as these texts were written from the standpoint of belief in God's intervention in history shaping the course of human events according to a preconceived plan.

We have seen that von Rad did not hesitate to view prophecy as a sharp break with earlier tradition, a departure so decisive that treatment of prophetic literature demanded a separate volume. His earlier attempt to deal with wisdom as Israel's response to God had drawn considerable fire, for Israel's sages can hardly be linked with sacral traditions of a chosen people. Von Rad felt the force of this criticism, and began a campaign that culminated in his important book, *Wisdom in Israel.*[2] Here he endeavored to prove that wisdom was another form of Yahwism.

THE OLD TESTAMENT WORLD VIEW

To accomplish his desired goal, von Rad needed to demonstrate that ancient Israel made no sharp distinction between nature and history. He therefore devoted considerable attention to Israel's world view, which he insisted differed greatly from the modern view of the world, and also contained a number of distinctive features in the ancient Near East.

I have used the singular, "world view," in talking about Israel's beliefs. Perhaps the plural form would have been more appropriate, for von Rad insists that Israel had more than one tenable view of the world. He does not explain what this means; if he thinks in terms of a single world view that is constantly in process of revision according to new experiences of reality, I can concur in his affirmation of more than one world view. If, on the other hand, he means several complete world views set over against one another, I must demur most resolutely.

Any discussion of world view must seek to determine at the outset what is unique to ancient Israel. Now much that belongs under Israelite world view is shared by Israel and the other peoples of the ancient Near East. Of course, this area of common belief is important. But von Rad focuses upon what is distinctive about Israel's view of the world. He does so for an important reason: faith and world view interpenetrate one another. In essence, Yahwism shapes its own world view, and is unthinkable in any other belief system.

The necessity to determine what is distinctive in Israel's belief about the world rules out a study of creation as the central idea or starting place.[3] Von Rad writes that Israel shares a belief in creation with all her neighbors, a point that has recently been developed by H. D. Preuss in an effort to prove that Israel's wisdom literature is paganism pure and simple.[4]

Another reason for rejecting creation as the starting point in ascertaining Israel's world view derives from the secondary role of creation in theological statements. Von Rad insists that creation faith in the Old Testament undergirds salvation history: creation proves Yahweh's power to save. In his view, the only exceptions to this supportive function of creation faith take place in psalms that have been borrowed from Israel's neighbors. It seems to follow that von Rad could have argued that relegating creation to a secondary and supportive role was distinctively Yahwistic, but he does not make much of this important fact in distinguishing between Israel and her neighbors.

Recent analysis of Israel's belief in creation has challenged von Rad's understanding of the soteriological function of creation. Hans Heinrich Schmid goes so far as to insist that creation lies at the very center of all theological thinking in Israel.[5] By identifying creation thinking with belief in order, Schmid succeeds in bringing the belief in creation into the center of daily activity. My own study of creation in hymnic and wisdom texts seems to confirm Schmid's hypothesis about the centrality of creation in theology,[6] but would also support von Rad's claim that creation functions in a subservient role. If I am correct, creation undergirds belief in God's justice.

Certainly, the form in which Israel describes creation differs little from that current among her neighbors. Three views can be discerned with minimal effort: procreation, creation by battle, and creation by word or fiat. The first hardly suits Yahwistic thought, for Israel's God had no consort. Echoes of this understanding of creation have survived in the Old Testament, chiefly in the epithet, "creator of heaven and earth," that seems to come from Canaanite sources. The Hebrew word for creator, *qanah*, can mean "to beget," but it also signifies "to acquire." In any event, the name of the first person born of woman (Cain) uses this root, and may conceal reminiscences of a procreational view of reality.

Another interpretation of the world's beginnings emphasizes a struggle between God and forces of chaos. Traces of this view appear in Job, Second Isaiah, and certain psalms. In this account, Yahweh conquers the great sea monster, whose name varies from Rahab to Leviathan and Tannin. In some versions, God sets limits within which this creature may cavort, while in others he slays the primordial dragon.

Still another view of creation stresses the origin of things as a result of divine fiat. God speaks and the world comes into existence. This priestly creation story (Gen. 1:1–2:4a) still bears marks of a different understanding of creation, namely by means of a battle in which God conquered Tiamat and Bohu, creatures representing chaos. Outside Israel, gods were also able to create by magical means, and thus primarily by a word.

It follows that Israel's accounts of creation held much in common with those of other peoples in the Fertile Crescent. This indisputable likeness in creation stories convinced von Rad that he should look somewhere else for a point of departure in discussing Israel's unique world view. He found that starting

point in Israel's prohibition against idols, which von Rad thinks
is fundamental to Yahwistic thought from the very earliest
period.

But what did Israel mean by this rejection of idols? In the
first place, she did not intend by this means to encourage spiritual worship or to discourage external worship that was linked
too closely with material objects. Von Rad notes that Israel did
not scorn the material world; on the contrary, she had the utmost regard for things of this world, which Yahweh bestowed
upon those who pleased him. Nowhere do we find evidence of
asceticism in Israel, he writes; the created order is wholly good,
and was pronounced so by its creator.

In reality, Israel was incapable of understanding idolatry.
Very few people actually identified the deity with the object
fashioned by hand. Instead, the worshiper understood the image
to be a revelation of the god. Somehow the deity communicated
himself or herself to the worshiper by means of this sacred
object. Von Rad writes:

> . . . in other words, by means of the cultic image there is en-
> counter between God and man. Without the gods, and without
> concrete representations of them, man would be lost in the world.
> Yet the mystery of godhead bursts out all around him.[7]

Idolatry was thus no survival of religious infantilism, but
merely drew logical conclusions from a conviction that deity is
experienced in ordinary events. Thus the idolater is immensely
tolerant, for all places and things are possible bearers of revelation. From this perspective, one easily sees why ancient critics
of Israel considered her irreligious.

Second, Israel's prohibition of images drew attention to God's
freedom to choose when and where he would make himself
known. It underscored divine sovereignty and left human beings

at the mercy of God. To make up for possible loss, Israel insisted that Yahweh was present in a personal sense, speaking the
living word and performing the historic act in behalf of his
people. Such assurance made lavish use of anthropomorphic
language; God was described in human categories. Von Rad
notices the enigma that follows from such language.

> The enigma of the divine revelation to Israel lies in the antinomy
> between the startling grandeur of its anthropomorphisms and the
> uncompromising strictness of its prohibitions of cultic images.[8]

Moreover, the rejection of images arose from a refusal to
view any part of the created world, or the sum total of it, as an
emanation of deity. Israel believed that the world was Yahweh's
handiwork; as such, it bears witness to the creator. Von Rad
remarks that the result is a radical purging of both the divine
and the demonic from the material universe.

Several consequences follow upon belief in a created order
distinct from God. First, Israel was barred from understanding
the world in terms of myth. Virtually all myths within the Old
Testament have been historicized; the only exception is the
story of the fallen angels in Genesis 6. Perhaps it would be
more accurate to say that every mythical element has been assimilated into Yahwistic thinking. Second, sex was not divinized
in Israel. Confronted by the mystery of sexuality, man and
woman neither withdrew from fear nor bowed in worship. The
coming together of man and woman was God's gift and command, but they need not look elsewhere for a means of assuring
that conception would result. This understanding of sex ruled
out cultic images and magical practices aimed at inducing preg-
nancy, for God personally saw to the consequences of sexual
union. Moreover, the realm of death lost something of its power,
for it, too, was at God's command. Such demythologization of

death never proceeded as far as to bring Yahweh into direct relationship with the realm of the dead.

CREATION'S WITNESS TO THE SILENT ONE

Although neither the world nor any part of it can be coaxed into mediating Yahweh's presence, the created order is not mute. Von Rad freely admits that all of creation sings God's praise. The Israelite, he writes,

> lives within a created order from which ascends an unending hymn of praise, yet he himself hears nothing of it. . . . He must be taught, as if he were blind and deaf, that he lives in a world which could be revealed to him, a world indeed in which, according to the remarkable teaching of Prov. viii, he is himself enfolded in the self-revealing secret of the created order.[9]

We shall take up this theme of a self-revealing universe at a later time, inasmuch as it assumes paramount importance in von Rad's discussion of wisdom.

In effect, von Rad claims that Yahweh controls nature as well as history. Even this language approaches a level of abstraction that was entirely foreign to Israel, he avers: "All these notions —Nature, sickness, death, history and so on—are merely vast ciphers, so many images projected as it were on a cinema-screen which separates God from man."[10] To see the world as Israel saw it, one must cast off mythical and philosophical ways of thinking.

To begin with, we must recognize that Israel knew nothing about a cosmos, an order of the universe with its own inherent laws to which Yahweh was subject. Just as he controlled events on the political arena, so God exercised complete authority over nature as well. To be sure, Israel spoke of laws governing the universe, but she believed that God was sovereign over even these rules. The world depended upon God for its very existence, as Psalm 104 declares so eloquently.

In Israel's view, Yahweh not only controlled ordinary natural events, such as the seasons, the sending of rain, dew, and snow, but he also determined when earthquakes and similar catastrophes would strike an unsuspecting and vulnerable populace. Calamity functioned to punish sinful humanity; in short, nature often carried out God's disciplinary or punitive task. Such disaster that accompanied natural upheavals did not ordinarily discriminate between good and evil victims. Instead, a principle of preponderance operated. After collective thinking gave way to individualistic emphasis, protest filled the heavens. When sin's burden weighed heavily upon a whole community or nation, punishment fell upon guilty and innocent alike. Still, the supreme instance of natural calamity, the flood, did not prevail over one righteous man and his family, which may indicate that Israel's thinkers early recognized a problem in the indiscriminate destruction brought about by natural calamity.[11]

Despite the punitive role of nature, Israel refused to complain to God about the world. Von Rad remarks that the Old Testament is brimful of complaints, but not one concentrates on the material universe. Instead, these protests strike out at the God who stands behind the world and employs it to accomplish his purposes. Over and over, the complaint psalms lash out at personal enemies and accuse God of blindness, inattention to justice, unfaithfulness to his promises, and kindred offenses. Even within the most caustic onslaught against God, the Book of Job, the world escapes unsullied. God, on the other hand, receives the full brunt of a frontal assault on his integrity. Ironically, God points to the wonders of nature as eloquent witness to his impartial justice. Perhaps it would be better to say that they proclaim his godhead, for justice hardly describes the God of Job.

These divine speeches concentrate upon the unfathomable character of the universe. Men and women can only touch the hem of God's garment; indeed, in this primordial world they did not even exist. By such means, Job is divested of the illusion of the central position.[12] Human knowledge can only play on the perimeters of divine mystery. How ludicrous, therefore, is Job's implicit claim that he has sufficient wisdom and virtue to equip him for the task of governing the universe.

Such reflection upon the secrets of the Lord that lie hidden within the core of the universe may evoke worship or despair. Von Rad recognizes the necessity of faith in such an awe-full universe. "His world was surely more abyssal than the one which shelters under our term 'Nature,' and only he who kept his eyes upon its Maker and Ruler could either comprehend it or endure it." [13] Whereas some people saw divine mystery as comforting, others decried an inability to search out what God had hidden. Von Rad perceives a strand of resignation even within such a story as the Joseph narrative, which affirms God's control of human events and natural disaster to accomplish his hidden purpose. That veil of resignation is drawn tightly shut in the brief sayings of Agur (Prov. 30:1–4) and Ecclesiastes.

Refusal to adopt a dualistic understanding of the universe cost Israel a great price. Yahweh's hand was seen in "every kind of political folly, military catastrophe, disease, earthquake, famine, drought or locust plague." Israel's response was a combination of anger and bewilderment; "still the psalm rode roughshod over the sufferer's bewilderment: 'it is Yahweh and none other who forms light and creates darkness, makes weal and creates woe; I am Yahweh, who do all these things.' " [14]

The attempt to view God as active in nature and history produced a significant problem: a nature world view that tends to universalize, whereas history particularizes. Because the Old Testament makes no distinction between the two, tension mounts. Von Rad examines various tradition complexes to ascertain the degree of tension concerning the issue of particularism and universalism, and reaches some remarkable conclusions.

The priestly narrative begins with the creation of the world, surely a universalistic stance, but concludes with an account of the Tabernacle, which represents a particularistic concern. No sign of tension between the two exists in the text. The Yahwist, on the other hand, resolves the tension by adopting a grandiose plan by which the family of Abraham will bring God's blessing to all humanity.

Von Rad observes that certain universalistic texts have been touched up by editors who wished to include the particularistic claim of Yahwistic faith. For example, Psalm 19 tells of the universe's unending song that is pitched too high for human ears, but a final gloss praises torah, a revelation that is accessible to humankind. Similarly, Job 28 speaks of God's wisdom that was built into the very structure of the universe, but men and women cannot discover it. Here, too, an editor finds a way out of universalistic gloom: God's wisdom and the fear of the Lord, that is, religion, are identical.

In Proverbs 8 wisdom is represented as the instinct of the universe, the secret of creation. But this answer does not suffice, von Rad remarks, since wisdom must reveal herself anew although she existed in the beginning of creation. A wholly new departure takes place in Ecclesiasticus 24, where wisdom has sought a dwelling place without success, and finally settles upon Jerusalem. Here we have a fall, von Rad claims, comparable to the old story in Genesis 3. In all these texts Israel endeavored to bring together two manifestations of God: nature and history.

Just as nature and history were kept together in ancient Israel, so also faith and knowledge complemented one another. Far from hindering understanding, religious faith set the intellect free to grasp overwhelming mystery. Von Rad refuses to budge an inch on this important matter, regardless of modern claims to the contrary. Although his intention is not to endorse ancient views and to urge their substitution for contemporary ones, he does insist that modern values and comprehensions must not pronounce judgment upon their ancient counterparts.

What was the nature of Israel's thought processes? Von Rad distinguishes between two types of knowledge, one of which he calls philosophy and the other gnomic apperception. The latter derives from everyday experience, and represents the distillation of truth garnished from careful study of reality. Couched in brief, poetic form, this knowledge is self-validating. Whoever hears the aphorism perceives immediately and intuitively that it encapsulates a certain truth that is worthy of preserving.

This kind of thinking does not take second place on the scale of intellectual rigor, but demands the very best from those who would engage in its discriminating task. Recognizing that at best one can only arrive at partial truth, gnomic thinking allows as many voices to join in the melody being played as humanly possible. The result is a stereometric kind of thinking, according to which a subject is looked at from any number of perspectives. By insisting on ever-widening perceptions, this form of thought hopes to capture the complexity of a given idea.

The poetic idiom enhances such stereometry. Hebrew poetry uses highly sophisticated parallelism, chiefly of three kinds: synonymous, antithetic, and ascending or cumulative. Whether varying the idea only slightly by use of synonymous concepts, or stressing direct opposition, or heaping up related ideas that throw light upon the topic from all sides, the poet enlarges the scope of perception. A single example suffices. In Proverbs 1:2–7, a sage has attempted to describe the goal of all learning, and thus to commend this particular collection of proverbs. The passage teems with pregnant terms, none of which is adequately defined here or anywhere else: wisdom, instruction, insight, righteousness, prudence, knowledge, discretion, proverb, figure, riddle, and so forth.

In addition to stereometric proclivities, gnomic thinking rests upon a fundamental presupposition that human events are analogous to natural ones. Actually, wisdom thinking can be described as a search for analogies. By examining the realm of ordinary experience, the wise hope to discover the secrets of the universe itself, and thus to penetrate beyond the surface of things to their essence. But von Rad is quick to point out that the secrets of the universe are in truth Yahweh's mystery which he has concealed within nature, since his glory is to hide things (Prov. 25:1).

This quest to uncover analogies lays bare the highly ambivalent character of all knowledge. Israel's sages came face to face with the relative aspect of all perceived truths. Silence was appropriate in some situations, and inexcusable in others. Poverty was proof of laziness at times, and at other times it fell into the category of divine agent to test those he loved. Moreover, the sages came to grasp the ambivalence of certain psychological states, particularly shame.

This confrontation with knowledge's ambivalence forced sages to recognize that they could never be absolutely certain. The result was a tendency toward caution and an aversion to sweeping explanations. Experience taught the wise that they had to take into consideration ad hoc divine actions that overruled valid laws governing the world. Von Rad contrasts the modern puzzlement over irregularities in the world with ancient Israel's radical astonishment over the discovery of laws regulating things.

In one sense, all knowledge represented an attempt to understand the self, whether in relation to ordinary reality or to divine mystery. But in another respect, every understanding of the world and self returns to the question about commitment to God. Even the notion of folly was a moral one at heart. The fool lacked ethical character; his impoverishment was more religious than intellectual. Such a person refused to acknowledge inherent natural laws encountered in experience; instead, he adamantly insisted on ignoring or rejecting what others had found to be valid.

Von Rad denies that the sages ever developed a dogma of retribution. It follows that they did not undergo a crisis resulting from a collapse of the conviction that God rewarded virtue and punished vice, since this belief never hardened into dogma. In order to maintain his position, von Rad has to downplay the impact of Job and Ecclesiastes upon the sages. Such a thesis lacks cogency, in my judgment.

On the other hand, von Rad's refusal to view certain proverbs as doctrinaire enables him to concentrate on the liberating power of knowledge. No force in heaven or on earth can frustrate Yahweh's plans for his creatures. This includes human notions of order. God remains free to protect men and women from their own plans. Von Rad marvels at Israel's ability to rest content with the world, in which she felt fully at home. Even the severe restrictions on human knowledge generated little anxiety, he thinks, since Israel knew God to be well disposed toward his creatures.

The sages never tired of speaking about the self-revealing universe. Ever wooing men and women, the universe never fully discloses its mystery. Still, the world order advances toward people and asks to be loved. Furthermore, this revelatory principle of the universe turns primarily toward individuals rather than whole nations. Von Rad concedes that this idea comes close to a mystical experience:

If there was, somewhere in Israel, a surrender, verging on the mystical, of man to the glory of existence, then it is to be found in these texts which can speak of such a sublime bond of love between man and the divine mystery of creation. Here man throws himself with delight on a meaning which rushes towards him; he uncovers a mystery which was already on its way to him in order to give itself to him.[15]

An essential ingredient of wisdom consisted in recognizing the correct time for a particular word or deed. A science of times grew up in the ancient world: Egyptian and Mesopotamian sages endeavored to determine the future and to recognize good and bad omens. Israel's sages understood the importance of timeliness, but their conviction that God held the future in his capable hands ruled out a science of reading the signs of the times. Instead, these wise men and women concentrated on discerning propriety in interpersonal relations.

Von Rad interprets this rejection of attempts to determine—and thus control—the future as one of several indications that Israel's sages had outgrown the cult. His denigration of the role of cultic themes in Ecclesiasticus flies in the face of considerable evidence to the contrary; one would have thought that von Rad's acknowledgment of the survival of archaic cultic ideas about medicine and physicians would have forced him to reexamine the bold statement that Sirach was interested only in the moral preconditions for ritual activity. On the complex problem of wisdom and cult, Leo G. Perdue's recent monograph provides a much needed corrective to von Rad's negative assessment.[16]

Not all Israel's sages felt at home in the world. In some ways, von Rad's penetrating analysis of man on the attack against God represents one of the most cogent interpretations of Job, Ecclesiastes, and Ecclesiasticus that has appeared to this date. He prefaces the attack with the word *trust*. In his view, the two

ideas, trust and attack, go together. Precisely because Job and
Ecclesiastes knew that God invited expostulation, they spoke
freely. Von Rad makes an important point in this context: the
modern interpreter must guard against assuming that ancient
readers would have regarded religious rebels with the same
favor that we do.

As a consequence of profound conviction that God was trustworthy, the sages succeeded in promulgating a positive understanding of suffering. They taught that God trains his people in
the same way teachers introduce their students to rigorous
learning. Just as a rod, freely used, assured success in the educational enterprise, so discipline from above guaranteed spiritual growth. Von Rad concedes that the idea of divine testing
crops up here and there outside the wisdom literature, particularly in the Elohistic narrative and in Second Isaiah, but he
insists that the wise bring this notion to fruition.

From one perspective, the Book of Job pictures a divine
test: God permits the Satan to submit Job to a severe test, and
all the while God and the heavenly court await Job's response
with bated breath. Von Rad remarks that God's gamble would
have failed if Job had uttered a different response. Had Job
closed his mind to God's final speech from the whirlwind, Satan
would have won the wager. In trying to grasp the theological
import of this book, von Rad has great difficulty reconciling the
old prose story with the poetic dialogue. Like many other interpreters, he severs the two segments of the book.

As von Rad sees it, the fundamental issue confronting Job
concerns a problematical God rather than suffering. Is Yahweh
for me or against me? This question forces itself upon Job
with crushing force. Here for the first time, von Rad writes,
Yahweh presses upon his trusted servant as a personal enemy,
returning harsh blows for a life of complete devotion.

Surprisingly, von Rad emphasizes Job's dependence upon

ancient cultic dialogues with God, and acknowledges the link with old Yahwistic traditions. In this respect, Job was closer to Yahwism than his three friends who sought to comfort him by appealing to religious tradition. By resting his case upon Yahwistic tradition, Job breaks with wisdom.

The author of Ecclesiastes strikes von Rad as one who has abandoned all hope of achieving dialogue with the tradition or God. Three themes characterize his thinking: everything is vanity; God determines every event; and man cannot discern God's decrees. Despite death's shadow, which hovers over every sentence of the book, von Rad views the work as an enthusiastic endorsement of life. Nevertheless, he accuses the author of giving up vital dialogue in favor of a monologue of an outsider who has freed himself from tradition. Having lost faith, he no longer struggles toward mastering life. Here we encounter one who has been thrown back upon his own resources, and has found them wanting. Like a horrible monster, the world presses in upon this pitiable figure and challenges him to a duel for which he has no stomach.

From these observations it becomes clear why von Rad rejects Walther Zimmerli's thesis that Ecclesiastes functions as a guardian of authentic Yahwism—God's freedom.[17] Zimmerli, professor of Old Testament at Göttingen, and best known for his massive commentary on Ezekiel and to English readers for two books, *The Law and the Prophets*, and *Man and his Hope in the Old Testament*,[18] saw Ecclesiastes as the product of a crisis in Israel's intellectual history. Since von Rad rejects the prevalent theory that ambiguous experience precipitated a crisis in Israel's belief system, he cannot very well view Ecclesiastes as the courageous thinker who called Israel back to a conviction that Yahweh acts in complete freedom.

Von Rad does admit that Job's friends left Yahweh little room to maneuvre, or rather, surrounded themselves with a wall of that which cannot be explained. But he prefers to see limits imposed upon reason as occasions for genuine worship. Accordingly, he interprets comparable attacks upon God's justice, such as Psalms 37, 49, and 73, as profound trust in the face of apparent injustice.

A single theme runs through this whole discussion of trust and attack. Von Rad wants to show what a small step it was from knowledge to adoration. Praise crops up in wholly unexpected places. Condemned criminals speak a doxology of judgment, and a guilty people praises God in the midst of punishment. Since Von Rad's next to last published essay is titled, "Doxology of Judgment." [19] we shall probe the theme a bit more fully.

THE DOXOLOGY OF JUDGMENT

The study of praise amidst adversity represents a longstanding interest. In discussing certain prophetic texts, von Rad had adopted Friedrich Horst's term, doxology of judgment.[20] Perhaps best known for his contributions to our understanding of Israel's law, but also for a commentary on Job that death cut short, Horst wrote an important essay on hymnic passages in Amos and labeled them doxologies of judgment. On the basis of ritual procedure outside Israel, he claimed that Israelites also knew confessions in the face of a death sentence. Horst appealed to the story of Achan, specifically to the injunction that he give glory to God (Josh. 7:19). From this sound base, Horst endeavored to strengthen his argument by interpreting other texts as judgment doxologies (from Job in particular).

Von Rad enlarges this textual foundation for doxologies of judgment. In many respects, his additional texts agree with those I have sought to interpret in this light. My own study of the doxologies in Amos (4:13; 5:8–9; 9:5–6), *Hymnic Affirmation of Divine Justice*, sought to broaden Horst's exegetical base to include, among other texts, Daniel 9, Ezra 9, and Nehemiah 9. Whereas I was interested primarily in thematic elements, von Rad seems to limit his attention to confessional patterns and to the picture of Israel's history that surfaces.

In Ezra 9:6–15 the speaker acknowledges guilt from the beginning of Israel as a people and praises God for leniency. Nehemiah 9 begins with a doxology (v. 6), and gives a more detailed survey of Israelite history. Here, too, Yahweh is lauded as righteous, and Israel's guilt is admitted. In Daniel 9:4–19, emphasis falls on past disobedience and refusal to heed prophetic voices. To the Lord belongs righteousness, and to Israel, shame. Similarly, Baruch 1:15–3:8 begins with confession of God's justice, to which a dark history of sin unfolds as a sharp contrast. Von Rad recognizes certain peculiarities in this text: dependence upon earlier prophetic passages, and a vow in 3:6–7.

Concluding that these highly similar passages derive from one author or a stable theological tradition complex, von Rad searches for a historical crisis when Israel knew herself to be under divine judgment. Rejecting the fall of Jerusalem in 587 B.C.E. as the crisis in question, since no serious reflection on that event occurs in these texts, he notes the similarities with 2 Esdras 3:4–27, which views Israel's history as a complete failure.

Von Rad also asks questions about the form of these texts. He views them as literary texts rather than cultic ones. Daniel 9 takes us to a scholar's study, while Baruch 1–3 comprises part of a letter. Still, ritual form imposes itself upon the texts in a forceful manner: an individual utters a *collective* prayer. In addition, the confession of Yahweh's righteousness (cf. 2 Chron. 12:6) is an essential component of a cultic form, which is confirmed by Lam. 1:18.

These facts lead von Rad to the conclusion that a service of repentance and fasting arose in ancient Israel, one in which calamity prompted her to recall past sins, accept punishment, and absolve God. In this manner Israel celebrated doxologically God's righteousness over against the sinfulness of all creatures. Von Rad recalls 1 Kings 8:33 ff., which enjoins thanksgiving under duress, and thinks that particular ritual is indeed a doxology of judgment.

Not every one of these texts contains a specific confession of Yahweh's righteousness. Is it possible that such declaration can be dispensed with in the doxology of judgment? Von Rad seems to answer this question affirmatively, and thus widens his net to include Nehemiah 1:5–11 and certain post-canonical texts (Ps. Sol. 8:7; 9:2; 17:10; Assmp. M. 3:5; Psalms from Qumran 12:31; 14:18; 17:20).

From this point, von Rad ventures forth to an examination of Tobit's death wish (Tobit 1:3–3:6). Here Tobit prays for death, but confesses that God is righteous. Obviously, von Rad faces a real problem here: how do a judgment doxology, acknowledgment of judgment, request for forgiveness, and implicit request for an end to punishment relate to a death wish? As we might expect, von Rad answers his question in terms of powerful restrictions imposed by the form upon the author of the story. Another difficulty bothers von Rad: does a doxology of judgment ever refer to an individual? Surely, he writes, the background of this text is the practice of setting up votive stelae on occasions of extreme misery.

Precisely what did a repentant one say in a doxology of judgment? Since Josh. 7:19 does not inform us what Achan said, von Rad looks elsewhere. In Exodus 9:27–28, he finds appropriate words placed in the mouth of a pharaoh: "I have sinned this time; the Lord is in the right, and I and my people are in the wrong." It follows, in von Rad's judgment, that execution did not necessarily accompany a judgment doxology.

Von Rad now turns to Job 5:8–16 and 33. He dismisses the former as useless, since it is not a single literary unit. But the latter text provides an important example of a cultic ceremony. On the basis of these texts, von Rad argues for the existence of a festival of lament in later Israel. Whether the advice to Job belongs to sacral law must be tested by the texts themselves, von Rad warns. In resolving this issue, one must make a careful analysis of thanksgiving songs of the individual, as well as those sin offerings and votive stelae that praise various deities for gracious response to a guilty petitioner.

THE AGONY AND ECSTASY OF THE BELIEVER

Whatever else we learn from the doxology of judgment, one thing stands out with special brilliance: the chaos that befalls men and women emanates from their own conduct. Von Rad never tires of emphasizing Israel's conviction that the world was worthy of trust, and vindicated it. Furthermore, false trust led to one's total destruction.

Nowhere do we find this teaching with greater clarity than in Ecclesiasticus, where Sirach wrestles with a group of skeptics set on refuting any notion of divine justice. Von Rad's insights in this regard demonstrate exceptional understanding of the way Sirach went about defending God's governance of the universe. Indeed, my own attempt to throw some light on this vexing problem owes much to von Rad's perception of Sirach's new departure in this area.[21]

Just how does Sirach endeavor to refute his antagonists? Essentially, he makes use of all the traditional arguments in support of God's justice that Walther Eichrodt discussed so ably in his great legacy to Old Testament interpretation, *Theology of the Old Testament*.[22] But Sirach does not stop here; instead, he conjectures that even God's intervention in the human arena is ambivalent. Von Rad rightly recognizes this as a wholly new kind of argument in justifying God's ways.

What von Rad neglects to point out is that Sirach's struggle with dissenters gives birth to two radically different arguments from earlier ones. Both defy verification or refutation. Sirach sought refuge in the realms of metaphysics and psychology. He claimed that the universe itself fought in behalf of virtuous persons, rewarding them and punishing the wicked mercilessly. The other argument insisted that sinners possessed a lion's share of anxiety. In short, God punished them with psychological stress, particularly by means of nightmares. In both arguments, Sirach demonstrates the truth of the claim that he represents a transition in Israelite wisdom. Here talk about contact with Greek thought becomes more than idle conjecture.

So far, our discussion of Israel's world view has relied almost entirely upon wisdom literature, except for the analysis of the prohibition against idols. To avoid misunderstanding, we must insist that von Rad has much to say elsewhere about one aspect of Israel's world view—the belief that God encounters his people in the course of human events. This conviction shaped prophetic messages and provided controlling rubrics in the writing of Israel's history.

Although nurtured in various sacred traditions, Israel's prophetic witnesses united in the conviction that God shaped political events for good or ill. This sense of destiny filled their messages to the brim, and increased the urgency in their warnings. In addition, it gave rise to the hope that some day God's kingdom would become living reality.

Israel's "historians" also believed that God controlled political events, and they sought diligently to make sense of Israel's checkered history. As we have seen, they imposed their own arbitrary pattern upon those events, but in so doing they hoped to call a chastened people back to straight paths. Fully embued with the prophetic spirit, these "historians" hoped to demonstrate the power of God's word.

Where does treatment of apocalyptic works like Daniel, Isaiah 24–27, Zechariah 9–14 and similar texts belong? Do they concur with the prophetic understanding of history, or does their view of the determination of times mark them as children of wisdom? Von Rad dares to present the thesis that apocalyptic and wisdom share a common viewpoint.

According to him, apocalyptic thrusts God's saving event to the fringes of history, either in the primeval election and determination of decrees or in the anticipation of salvation at the end of time. No longer does God intervene in the regular course of history; instead, apocalyptists look backward to the creative act when God determined the destinies of all who would be born from that moment until the end of eternity. Or they glance forward to the great and final entry of God into the world when the forces of good and evil gather for the terrible battle that will engulf all mankind. Prophecy thinks in altogether different terms, von Rad argues, for it believes that history is always open to new possibilities. Only in this way can prophecy make sense of the dialectic between human response to God's judging deed and the divine reaction to this new situation.

This attempt to view apocalyptic as an outgrowth of wisdom thinking has met with sharp criticism.[23] That hostile reaction arises largely from two factors: the overwhelming similarities between prophecy and apocalyptic, and the numerous differences between apocalyptic and wisdom. Von Rad's idiosyncratic interpretation rests on too narrow a base, and for that reason is not likely to compel wide assent.

How can we sum up von Rad's discussion of Israel's world view? The principal observation we must make is that the world is created. From this fundamental statement flow many important consequences: no worship of idols, divinization of sex, mythologization of death, terror over demons. A second remark concerns what is certainly implicit in the first: God reigns as lord of nature and history, for these ciphers represent a unity in the mind of Israel's thinkers. A third observation speaks to the matter of priorities in a created world where a living God controls natural events and the course of history: faith liberates knowledge. If one wishes to know divine mystery, he must surrender to Him who holds the key to all knowledge. Finally, a fourth comment focuses upon the individual's experience of ambiguity: human response to such marvelous bounty as has been bestowed upon God's creatures is to join in the hymn of praise that creation itself sings from morning to night.

VI. From Tradition to the Silence of God

At all times and in every circumstance Israel occupied the middle ground between a prophecy and its fulfillment. Her literature seizes this important fact and describes saving history as a march toward God's final fulfillment of his promise to his people. Eschatology, it follows, is built into the very fabric of Israel's thinking about God's ways of dealing with her. No hour is too dark, no suffering too extreme, to erase that hope of final redemption.

The historical character of the Old Testament underlines this anticipation of a decisive act in the future. Von Rad writes that the Old Testament is a history book. According to our understanding, history moves toward a distant goal. Here he contrasts Israel's linear understanding of history, taken over by Western civilization, with the cyclical view endorsed by Israel's neighbors.

Furthermore, Israel's faith was constantly driven forward by the course of history, which always pointed ahead. Even the telling and retelling of God's saving deeds emphasized the openness of the future, and stories about redemptive acts invited repetition. In particular, God's promises directed all eyes to their future realization.

In von Rad's view, this forward looking leads directly to the threshold of the New Testament. In light of this bold claim, we shall examine the relationship between the two Testaments more thoroughly.[1] Perhaps the tone for such discussion is best set by a look at what von Rad describes as the supreme analogy between the Old and New Testament.

This analogy consists of a terrifying revelation: men are confronted more and more painfully with a God who withdraws, leaving them to gamble in faith. Israel's greatest burden was this tendency of God to hide from those who trusted him. In both Testaments God revealed himself as one who conceals himself at the same time that he discloses the mystery of his person. The life of Jesus and the crucifixion represent the ultimate in God's hiddenness, and Christians are expected to stake their lives on a crucified one.

The God who hides from those who trust him constantly makes promises, teasing Israel, as it were, with partial fulfillments. Still, God's people refused to allow a single promise to come to naught. As a result, expectation mounts unbearably.

Now it is certainly possible to argue that the Old Testament points directly into a void, and thus to understand saving history as aborting. Israel's theologians refused to entertain such a thought, but busily pumped new content into every divine promise. Each generation read something new into old stories, and thus revitalized them for another day.

For example, patriarchal tradition borrowed a tale about a river demon and applied it to Jacob as a means of forcing a transformation in his character before the dreaded confrontation with Esau took place. The prophet Hosea alludes to this same story, but introduces an entirely different interpretation of the wrestling match. Here Jacob prevails over God (Hos. 12:3–6).

In one area, in particular, constant reinterpretation radically altered initial reflections. That rapidly changing perspective dealt with the anointed one, that enigmatic figure who will bring God's promises to David into full fruition. If we ask precisely what the Messiah will be like, a number of responses present themselves. That marvelous anointed one will be a king, a suffering servant, a prophet like Moses, a Spirit-endowed leader. In reality, each age described the coming one in terms of its own comprehension of the religious situation.

Such adaptation of previous traditions demonstrates remarkable freedom in handling sacred texts and revered tradition. Often this liberty pushed to extreme limits, even to questioning old saving events by substituting new ones. At other times, earlier themes assume altogether different meanings. In Proverbs, personified Wisdom issues a cordial invitation to all who desire knowledge, and Jesus borrows her language in summoning followers to come to him and take on his yoke.[2]

In still another way, the Old Testament lays the foundation for the New. It performs a preparatory function in the formation of a linguistic system that unites Jew and Christian. Both words and ideas span the two literary complexes, so that one trained in reading the Old Testament immediately understands the claim that the word became incarnate. So, too, that reader versed in Old Testament language perceives the mystery of a hidden God. Von Rad writes: "The fact that it was possible to speak of him in a manner which outraged pious feeling, and that this was, indeed, essential if the people were to see him as he really was, indicates how deeply he had withdrawn."[3] In this connection, we should note that von Rad does not think Israel's bondage to the law drove a wedge between her and God. On the contrary, she believed herself capable of fulfilling the law, for which she thanked God. Faith foundered on Yahweh's will to save, rather than upon the law.

Although the two Testaments make use of a common religious language, this is not what links them indissolubly. That powerful bond rests in the concept of saving history that fills each to the brim. Of course, the unity of the Old and New Testament depends upon typology. By this term, von Rad means a kind of analogical thinking that makes it possible to speak of type and antitype.[4] Earlier thinkers spoke more than they understood, and every saving event is pregnant. Fraught with potential, the wondrous word or deed occasions partial fulfillment at its first occurrence. But that event surfaces later in fuller dimension, and thereby lifts the veil further still.

Typological thinking does not provide occasion for equation of the two Testaments willy-nilly. Many New Testament allusions to the Old Testament constitute spur-of-the-moment linkages rather than legitimate proof from scripture. For this reason, von Rad rejects the conclusions arrived at in these New Testament texts. He goes a step further and insists that both Testaments need one another for legitimation. In particular, the New Testament needs the universalism inherent within the Old Testament's view of creation.

Another way to describe the *essential* link between the two Testaments is to emphasize the *credendum*. Von Rad believes that the typical element in every generation of God's people was the affirmation of faith. Despite repeated breaks in God's saving deeds, Israel confessed faith in the one who promised and stood behind that word to bring it from shadow to substance. This astonishing transformation took place over and over in the Old Testament, so that one would be mistaken in thinking that the New Testament alone has real substance.

To sum up, the Old Testament lays a foundation for the New by providing a religious language, the essential character of which was confessional and the substance, God's saving deeds in history. Beyond that, the Old Testament believer comes face to face with one who retreats ever more, and hence points forward to the mystery that defies all comprehension—the cross. In the Christian saving event, too, one encounters the silence of God.

Truly, the sojourner Israel ventured forth in faith from a foreign land into one through which she walked as an alien and from which she was driven, again to dwell like a stranger in a foreign land. As von Rad sees it, such is the lot of the believer— to watch helplessly as God, in whom one places full trust, increasingly hides himself in mystery until the voice that echoed through eternity becomes still again.[5]

VII. Gerhard von Rad:
Theologian and Exegete

ABIDING CONTRIBUTIONS

When Gerhard von Rad joined the ranks of Old Testament scholars, Harnack's negative assessment of the Hebrew scriptures had borne rich fruit. Surging national consciousness prompted a movement to replace Old Testament stories with German legends in the curriculum for preschool children.[1] The Hebrew background of the New Testament and Christianity was either ignored or denigrated, and anyone was suspect who viewed the Old Testament as theologically significant for the church. So powerful was this ethos that those few scholars who took a stand against it spoke from *within* the framework of national or *Volk* consciousness. Von Rad waged battle against this prevalent attitude to the Hebrew Bible, but his book on *The People of God in Deuteronomy* gave unconscious expression to the overwhelming sense of national consciousness in Germany.[2]

Still, von Rad's contribution in the struggle to regain the Old Testament for the Christian church is second to no one's. The powerful exegesis of text after text demonstrated beyond doubt the theological profundity of Old Testament confessions of faith. Von Rad's conscious use of *kerygma* and *credo* called attention to the fundamental character of such confessional statements. *Kerygma,* that is, belonged to the discourse of Old Testament interpretation just as much as it did to New Testament scholarship. In short, the prominent place the Hebrew Bible occupies in the church today is largely due to impetus set into motion by Gerhard von Rad.[3]

At the turn of the century, Old Testament scholarship had reached a kind of stalemate. The search for layers of literary sources had virtually exhausted the possibilities, all the time shifting attention away from the final product. Historians of religion, on the other hand, managed to illuminate the mythical stages of the material with remarkable success. They, too, focused upon the origins of the stories that comprised larger units without giving a moment's consideration to the comprehensive meaning of the final form. Thus some important essays by Hermann Gunkel were published in English with the title, *What Remains of the Old Testament.*[4]

In addition, three alternative approaches to the biblical text characterized German scholarship in general: fundamentalism, skepticism, and pneumatic exegesis. The first endorsed history as the basic category of revelation, and readily granted the historicity of the Old Testament at every point. Its opposite, skepticism, denied the historicity of crucial Old Testament narratives. A third perspective, the charismatic or spiritual, viewed the Old Testament as a prototype of the New. By means of typological interpretation, spiritual exegetes managed to salvage the Hebrew scriptures.

These powerful hermeneutical principles left their mark on von Rad in spite of his attempt to escape their clutches. Still, he added distinctive features to each one's impact, and thereby reduced the cumulative effect. Although he accepted history as the essential category of Old Testament revelation, von Rad re-

fused to equate history and faith. His students (Rolf Rendtorff
and Wolfhart Pannenberg) may have launched an attempt to
establish faith historically,[5] but von Rad never went that route.
On the contrary, he moved much closer to a skeptical stance in
regard to what scholars could actually know about historical
events. Nevertheless, von Rad insisted that Israel's confessional
statements were grounded in real events. The claim of pneumatic
exegesis upon von Rad came in an essay on typological interpretation of the Old Testament, as well as in the discussion of the
relationship between the two Testaments. A decisive difference
occurs here, too. Von Rad introduced the idea of promise and
fulfillment within *each* Testament.

How did von Rad hope to salvage the Hebrew Bible and to
introduce vitality into exegesis without adopting an approach
that betrayed the text? It occurred to him that the only appropriate way to do Old Testament theology was to let Israel's own
confessions determine the content of theology. In his judgment,
no systematic interpretation of the Old Testament could do
justice to the material, since it would not have been recognized
by Israel herself. Thus he developed his unusual approach to
Old Testament theology: the study of Israel's own confessional
theological statements of God's action in leading his people to
a distant goal.

The study of traditions in the Old Testament brought into
clear focus the necessity for actualization of the Word in each
generation.[6] Von Rad marveled at the way ancient Israel brought
together disparate traditions and transformed them into new
traditions that spoke to changing historical situations. This
emphasis upon representation through telling the sacred story
underscored the importance of proclamation in the Old Testament. But von Rad did not stop here. Instead, he endeavored to
bridge the gulf between then and now, the task of theology and
homiletics.

When von Rad turned his attention to wisdom literature, he discovered a means of setting natural theology within a wholly new framework.[7] In this way he managed to incorporate wisdom within an Old Testament theology, a goal that had eluded earlier critics. The implications of this shift in perspective have yet to be worked out; one thing is certain, however—von Rad has shown the inadequacy of the usual tendency to dismiss wisdom as paganism and to ignore its profound message.

Since von Rad conceded that his Old Testament theology is actually a history of Israel's confessional statements, we need to emphasize his contribution to the history of religions. Even if others had already discovered the centrality of confessional statements in this discipline, as Friedrich Baumgärtel claimed,[8] von Rad's masterful execution of the task of tracing Israel's creedal statements and streams of tradition deserves highest praise.

No assessment of von Rad's contribution to Old Testament studies is complete without reference to his form critical analysis. Above all else, von Rad functioned as a form critic. Again and again he used this method to bring a biblical text to life so that it addressed the reader in an entirely different setting.

Finally, I wish to observe that von Rad taught us to read the Old Testament aesthetically. Entering a discipline that has lacked genuine literary analysis, for the most part, he did much in paving the way for an appreciation of the Old Testament as literature. He accomplished this important task in two ways: by providing a singular example of literary analysis on the succession document, and by the sheer brilliance of his poetic mind.

NEGATIVE FEATURES

Von Rad's staunchest supporters would readily concede that his approach to Old Testament theology has evoked considerable dissent, for it has certain real problems. Of course, the starting point must be the problem of history in von Rad's thought.[9] Anyone who labels himself a little historical monoman and describes the Old Testament as a historical book invites reflection on the adequacy of his use of the term. Responding to critics who accused him of unnecessary skepticism regarding actual history, von Rad insisted that confessional statements arose in history. Event preceded word, he claimed. Still, the discrepancy between what really happened (at the Reed Sea, for example, or at Jericho) and the confessional statement was considerable in von Rad's view. Thus the question arose and demanded satisfactory response: how does one reconcile the historical minimum achieved by modern historians with the theological maximum acquired in von Rad's analysis?

In a sense, von Rad's adoption of the form critical method precluded a positive assessment of historical accounts. By its very nature, form criticism is skeptical of the historical events preserved within textual units. Accordingly, traditions tell the reader very little about the real Moses, for example. Essentially, von Rad's historical interest lies in the development of traditions. That is, he writes a history of Israel's *faith assertions*.

Von Rad's claim that the historical credo came at the beginning rather than at the end of cultic communities has provoked considerable controversy. His reasons for an early dating of the three confessional statements within the Hexateuch lack cogency. Late expressions, in fact, have led others to see in them summary statements of saving history, and thus have demanded the conclusion that they mark the culmination of a long sacral process.[10] In short, von Rad's thesis has been turned on its head.

Although von Rad refused to search for a center of the Old Testament, he permitted the historical confessions to function as a norm by which all else within the Hebrew Bible was judged.[11] This assumption that only a certain view of history belongs to the real theology of ancient Israel led von Rad to dismiss apocalyptic, wisdom, and numerous poetic texts as peripheral material. Furthermore, it motivated him to view prophecy apart from the traditions contained in the historical books, although he did find a way to link the two literary complexes. In a word, he viewed the prophets as interpreters of earlier traditions. This led to ambiguity over the precise point at which a break occurred—between the Hexateuch and prophecy, or within prophecy (Jeremiah, Ezekiel, and Deutero-Isaiah). Furthermore, the difficult problem of false prophecy illustrates the danger of a norm derived from saving history. What happens when false prophets base their words solidly upon salvation history?

Still another hidden center functions as a norm for von Rad, specifically, the Book of Deuteronomy.[12] One would think that his method rules out such a norm by which all else is judged. Nevertheless the actualization of earlier traditions associated with the Deuteronomic reform provides a model for von Rad's description of what must have taken place time and again.

Precisely why did von Rad reject all conscious attempts to find unity within the Hebrew Bible? In his mind, the desire to locate a center in the Old Testament constituted the task of systematic theology. Desiring to permit the Israelite traditions to speak for themselves, von Rad stood resolutely against any imposition of modern concepts upon the Old Testament.

Still another problem with von Rad's approach concerns his preoccupation with cultic institutions, which prevented his full appreciation of the ethical insights within Israelite prophecy.[13] Von Rad's assumption that early Israel was characterized by pan sacralism shaped his interpretation of important religious documents. Surprisingly, he minimized the significance of the cultic reforms under Ezra, possibly because he wanted to contrast Judaism of this period with the New Testament faith community.

Von Rad's form critical method and poetic mind combined to produce contradictory impulses in his thought. The former emphasis broke apart competing traditions, often when the two may have existed together with minimal tension, and the latter brought the several traditions together in exquisite recital. Small wonder rigorous systematicians accused von Rad of muddled thinking. His defense against such charges strikes me as particularly appropriate: the Old Testament scholar must not be more precise than the materials with which he works.

Since von Rad has been accused of ignoring scholarship outside Germany, I cannot conclude this discussion of weaknesses in his approach without a word about his lack of dialogue with other scholars. One way of understanding this curious fact is to say that von Rad feared lest human voices would drown out the words contained within ancient texts.[14] Another explanation is that von Rad entered into dialogue without actual references to those whose views he was attacking or adopting,[15] but evidence for this interpretation is wanting. In my opinion, von Rad fell short in this respect, and could surely have profited greatly from wider reading, particularly in English. Hopefully, that provincial attitude is vanishing from German scholarship.

Gerhard von Rad saw himself as a Christian theologian. Conviction that the voice of ancient Israel could and must be heard by the Christian church inspired his listening to a biblical text. For many of us who have heard the chorus of ancient voices because of von Rad's surrender to the task of bridging the gap between then and now, his work stands as a monument of faith and faithfulness.

Notes

CHAPTER I

1. W. H. Schmidt, " 'Theologie des Alten Testaments' vor und nach Gerhard von Rad," *Verkündigung und Forschung*, 1972, pp. 1–25. Full publication information not given in the notes may be found in the bibliography.

2. See especially Hans Conzelmann, "Fragen an Gerhard von Rad," *Evangelische Theologie* 24 (1964):113–25; Friedrich Baumgärtel, "Gerhard von Rad's 'Theologie des Alten Testaments,' " *Theologische Literaturzeitung* 86 (1961): 801–815, 895–907; J. Philip Hyatt, "Were There an Ancient Historical Credo in Israel and an Independent Sinai Tradition?" pp. 152–70; D. G. Spriggs, *Two Old Testament Theologies*, 1976.

3. Julius Wellhausen, *Prolegomena to the History of Ancient Israel* (New York: World Publication Company, 1957) reprints this article.

4. Gerhard von Rad, "Antrittsrede von Gerhard von Rad," Sitzungberichte der Heidelberger Akademie der Wissenschaften, 1955/56, 1957, and G. von Rad, "Über Gerhard von Rad," in *Forscher und Gelehrter*, ed. W. E. Böhm (1966), pp. 17–18; also in *Probleme biblischer Theologie*, ed. Hans Walter Wolff (1971), pp. 659–61, particularly p. 660. See also Hans W. Wolff, "Gespräch mit Gerhard von Rad," in *Probleme biblischer Theologie*, pp. 648–58, and "Gerhard von Rad als Exeget," in *Gerhard von Rad: Seine Bedeutung für die Theologie*,

ed. H. W. Wolff, Rolf Rendtorff and Wolfhart Pannenberg (1973), pp. 9–20 for discussion of von Rad's academic career.

5. Gerhard von Rad, *Das Gottesvolk im Deuteronomium* (Theol. Diss., Erlangen, 1929).

6. Strongly influenced by Karl Barth, Nold contended that Christ was to be found in the church ("Where is our participation in Christ? Not in the university!") See Wolff, "Gespräch mit Gerhard von Rad," p. 649.

7. Gerhard von Rad, *Das Geschichtsbild des chronistischen Werkes* (1930). Procksch suggested the title "Geschichtsanschauung" (Historical View), but von Rad rejected it as too subjective. The resulting "Geschichtsbild" is virtually impossible to render into English.

8. Wolff, "Gespräch mit Gerhard von Rad," pp. 650–51.

9. Discussion of this little known essay can be found in James L. Crenshaw, *Prophetic Conflict,* Beihefte zur Zeitschrift für die alttestamentliche Wissenschaft, vol. 124 (Berlin: Walter de Gruyter, 1971), pp. 15–16.

10. Gerhard von Rad, "The Tent and the Ark," in *The Problem of the Hexateuch and other Essays,* pp. 103–124; "There Remains Still a Rest for the People of God: An Investigation of a Biblical Conception," in ibid., pp. 94–102; "Die falschen Propheten," in *Zeitschrift für die alttestamentliche Wissenschaft* 51 (1933):109–120; *Die Priesterschrift im Hexateuch,* Beiträge zur Wissenschaft vom Alten und Neuen Testament, vol. 65 (Stuttgart: W. Kohlhammer Verlag, 1934).

11. Gerhard von Rad, *Das Alte Testament—Gottes Wort für die Deutschen!* (Berlin: Klares Ziel [1], 1937; *Moses,* English translation, 1960; "The Form-Critical Problem of the Hexateuch," in *The Problem of the Hexateuch;* "Erwägungen zu den Königspsalmen," in *Zeitschrift für die alttestamentliche Wissenschaft* 58 (1940–41):216–22; "The Beginnings of Historical Writing in Ancient Israel," *Archiv für Kulturgeschichte* 32 (1944):1–42, also included in *The Problem of the Hexateuch,* pp. 166–204; "The Promised Land and Yahweh's Land in the Hexateuch," in *The Problem of the Hexateuch,* pp. 79–93; "The Basic Problems of a Biblical Theology of the Old Testament," *Theologische Literaturzeitung* 68 (1943):225–34.

12. Gerhard von Rad, *The Problem of the Hexateuch,* pp. 4–5.

13. Gerhard von Rad, *Erinnerungen aus der Kriegsgefangenschaft Fruhjahr 1945* (Neukirchen-Vluyn: Neukirchener Verlag, 1976).

14. M. E. Andrew, "Gerhard von Rad . . . a Personal Memoir," *Expository Times* 83 (1972):296–300.

15. A complete bibliography until 1971 has been provided by Konrad von Rabenau in *Studien zur Theologie der alttestamentlichen Über-*

lieferungen, ed. Rolf Rendtorff and Klaus Koch, pp. 163–74 and in *Probleme biblischer Theologie,* ed. Wolff, pp. 665–81.

16. Wolff, "Gespräch mit Gerhard von Rad," p. 656, asks whether it was accidental that the first evangelical theologian since Harnack chosen for membership in the Peace category of the *Order pour le merité* was one who took up Harnack's challenge to the Old Testament and successfully defended its place in the Christian canon.

17. Rendtorff and Koch, eds., *Studien zur Theologie der alttestamentlichen Überlieferungen,* p. 196; Wolff, ed., *Probleme biblischer Theologie;* Wolff, et al., eds., *Gerhard von Rad: Seine Bedeutung für die Theologie.*

18. See note 4.

19. In this text von Rad sees himself as one who has carried on Alt's life's work and who has taken up much of his teacher's incomparable spirit. He expresses profound gratitude for Alt's patience with the young "Privatdozent" and for the rigorous demands imposed upon the assistant. The bond is said to have continued until Alt's death. This experience under Alt's tutelage von Rad calls the most fortunate fact of his life.

20. See von Rad, "Über Gerhard von Rad," pp. 660–61, where he laments the loss of intellectual power that accompanies the passing of time, and particularly Wolff, "Gerhard von Rad als Exeget," pp. 13–14.

21. Wolff, "Gerhard von Rad als Exeget," p. 19.

22. Gerhard von Rad, *Predigt-Meditationem,* ed. Ursula von Rad (Göttingen: Vandenhoeck & Ruprecht, 1973). English translation, *Biblical Interpretations in Preaching,* trans. John E. Steely (Nashville: Abingdon, 1977). This valuable collection of sermonic meditations (as distinct from actual sermons) deals with numerous biblical texts (Gen. 4:1–16; 12:1–9; 16:1–16; 22:1–19; 32:22–33; 50:20; Josh. 1:1–19; 1 Kings 19:1–8; 2 Kings 5:1–19; 2 Chr. 20; Job 2:1–10; Pss. 32; 96; Isa. 40:3–8; 52:13–53:12; 61:1–3, 10–11; Jer. 29:4–14; 31:31–34; Hag. 2:1–9; Mal. 4:1–6; Heb. 4:1–11). See also von Rad's *Predigten,* 1972.

23. Wolff, "Gespräch mit Gerhard von Rad," p. 657.

24. Karl Rahner, "Gerhard von Rad," *Das Parlament* 35 (Aug. 26, 1972): 10.

25. According to Mrs. von Rad his favorite authors were Goethe, Hesse, Rilke, and von Hofmannsthal. An accomplished violinist, von Rad was particularly fond of Mozart, Schubert, and Beethoven.

26. The influence of Leonhard Rost was by no means negligible.

27. Norman W. Porteous, "Magnalia Dei," in *Probleme biblischer Theologie,* ed. Wolff, p. 418.

28. Wolff, "Gerhard von Rad als Exeget," pp. 9, 13–14.

29. Gerhard von Rad, preface to vol. 2, *Old Testament Theology*, 1965.

30. Wolff, "Gerhard von Rad als Exeget," pp. 9, 16–17, writes that tradition historical hypotheses were changeable but that the constant task was the clarification of the text. Wolff admits that the emphasis on tradition in all stages as a means to the depth dimension of the text remained unchanged.

31. See note 2.

32. Gerhard von Rad, "Antwort auf Conzelmanns Fragen," *Evangelische Theologie* 24 (1964) : 394.

33. Wolff, "Gespräch mit Gerhard von Rad," p. 656. This essay first appeared in *Vetus Testamentum Supplements* 3 (1955) : 293–301; see now "Job xxxviii and Ancient Egyptian Wisdom," in *The Problem of the Hexateuch*, pp. 281–91.

34. Wolff, "Gespräch mit Gerhard von Rad," p. 657.

35. Porteous, "Magnalia Dei," pp. 417–27.

36. This charge was made by Baumgärtel, "Gerhard von Rads 'Theologie des Alten Testaments,'" p. 812, and acceded to by von Rad according to Wolff, "Gespräch mit Gerhard von Rad," p. 657. Roland de Vaux, "Method in the Study of Early Hebrew History," in *The Bible in Modern Scholarship*, ed. J. Philip Hyatt (Nashville: Abingdon Press, 1965), pp. 15–17, writes that von Rad's work fits more properly in the category of a history of Israel's religion than a theology of the Old Testament.

37. Gerhard von Rad, *Weisheit in Israel*, 1970 (English translation, 1972). See the preface in particular, which is in many ways a remarkable confession that traditio-historical methods are not applicable to wisdom literature.

38. This admission came in a letter to Hans Walter Wolff. See Wolff, "Gerhard von Rad als Exeget," p. 18.

39. Porteous, "Magnalia Dei," pp. 422–23.

40. Ibid., p. 422.

41. Gerhard von Rad, "The City on the Hill," in *The Problem of the Hexateuch*, p. 241; originally published in *Evangelische Theologie* 8, (1948–49).

42. Rolf Rendtorff, "Die alttestamentlichen Überlieferungen als Grundthema der Lebensarbeit Gerhard von Rads," in Wolff, et al., *Gerhard von Rad: Seine Bedeutung für die Theologie*, pp. 25–27.

43. Ibid., pp. 25–26.

44. Baumgärtel, "Gerhard von Rads 'Theologie des Alten Testa-

ments,' " pp. 803–4, 895 (indeed throughout this stinging essay). See also Spriggs, *Two Old Testament Theologies*.

45. Porteous, "Magnalia Dei," p. 419.

46. Baumgärtel, "Gerhard von Rad's 'Theologie des Alten Testament,' " pp. 903–7.

47. Von Rad, *Old Testament Theology*, vol. 2, part III.

48. Von Rad, "The Form-Critical Problem of the Hexateuch," p. 38.

49. Above all, in the new edition of the commentary on Genesis; see Wolff, "Gerhard von Rad als Exeget," p. 17.

50. Wolfhart Pannenberg, "Glaube und Wirklichkeit im Denken Gerhard von Rads," in *Gerhard von Rad: Seine Bedeutung für die Theologie*, ed. Wolff, et al., pp. 41–42.

51. Gerhard von Rad, *Predigten*, p. 91.

52. Lothar Perlitt, "Die Verborgenheit Gottes," in *Probleme biblischer Theologie*, ed. Wolff, pp. 367–82.

53. Von Rad, *Das Gottesvolk im Deuteronomium*, 1929; *Deuteronomium Studien*, Forschungen zur Religion und Literatur des Alten und Neuen Testaments, vol. 58 (Göttingen: Vandenhoeck & Ruprecht, 1947), English translation, 1953; *Das fünfte Buch Mose, Deuteronomium, übersetzt und erklärt*, Das Alte Testament Deutsch, vol. 8 (Göttingen: Vandenhoeck & Ruprecht, 1964), English translation, 1966. See Siegfried Herrmann, "Die Konstruktive Restauration: Das Deuteronomium als Mitte biblischer Theologie," in *Probleme biblischer Theologie*, ed., Wolff, pp. 155–70.

54. Porteous, "Magnalia Dei," pp. 418–19.

55. This expression, while not an exact equivalent of what von Rad seems to have meant by such "Geschichtsbilder," is chosen as the least misleading of several possibilities. What is meant by the expression will become clear, I hope, in the discussion.

56. Gerhard von Rad, "Gerichtsdoxologie," in *Schalom: Studien zu Glaube und Geschichte Israels (Alfred Jepsen zum 70 Geburtstag)*, ed. Karl-Heinz Bernhardt (Stuttgart: Calwer Verlag, 1971), pp. 28–37.

CHAPTER II

1. Gerhard von Rad, *Der Heilige Krieg im Alten Israel*, rev. ed., 1958 (1st edition, 1951).

2. In one sense the Solomonic era plays for von Rad a role comparable to ethical monotheism in the thought of Wellhausen and Duhm. In each instance a decisive era stood over against what preceded and followed.

3. In my judgment, the evidence fails to support von Rad's claim that life before the age of David was wholly sacral. I cannot find any such emphasis in early sagas (for example, the Samson narrative) or in old wisdom.

4. Von Rad discusses the Solomonic Enlightenment in several contexts: *The Problem of the Hexateuch*, pp. 69, 198–204, 292–300.

5. Recent research on the Joseph narrative and the patriarchal stories has called into question the usual dating of these literary complexes, while the appropriateness of viewing the Succession Document as an apologetic for the Solomonic empire becomes less probable as discussions of that text proliferate.

6. The confessional statements have a history which interests von Rad more than the bare facts of the nation Israel.

7. Critics *do* question its sacral quality, and thus the term *holy* war. For recent discussions, see Patrick D. Miller, *The Divine Warrior in Early Israel* (Cambridge: Harvard University Press, 1973), and Rudolf Smend, *Yahweh War and Tribal Federation* (Nashville: Abingdon Press, 1970).

8. Martin Noth, "The Background of Judges 17–18," in *Israel's Prophetic Heritage*, ed. B. W. Anderson and Walter Harrelson (New York: Harper & Bros., 1962), pp. 68–85, perceived the powerful argument these stories provide for the monarchy in Israel as opposed to rule by judges.

9. Noth's important theory appeared in *Das System der zwölf Stamme Israels* (1930; reprint ed., Darmstadt: Wissenschaftliche Buchgesellschaft, 1966).

10. The *qatsin* was a chief or ruler, while a *moshia'* was a deliverer.

11. It occurs in Israelite and Egyptian wisdom.

12. The term *charisma* first entered Old Testament interpretation through appropriation of Max Weber's sociological analysis, and has since enjoyed wide usage to distinguish especially gifted persons from those who function by right of birth.

13. For what follows, see von Rad, *The Problem of the Hexateuch*, pp. 103–124.

14. Ibid., p. 103.

15. Both Odil Hannes Steck, "Theological Streams of Tradition," in *Theology and Tradition in the Old Testament*, ed. Douglas A. Knight (Philadelphia: Fortress Press, 1977), pp. 183–214, and Morton Smith, *Palestinian Parties and Politics that Shaped the Old Testament* (New York: Columbia University Press, 1971), discuss competing loyalties within the Old Testament, although from wholly different perspectives.

16. In *Das Geschictsbild des chronistischen Werkes* (1930). Despite

von Rad's theological analysis of Chronicles (the genealogies!), he views the work as an example of mental exhaustion. In his eyes, Judaism declined after the great prophets.

17. Hugo Gressmann, *Altorientalische Bilder* (Tübingen: J. C. B. Mohr, 1909), p. cxxxv.

18. This argument presupposes that the negative treatment of the episode arose at a subsequent period and functioned to elevate Moses at Aaron's expense. The present text bears witness to conflict within the priestly hierarchy.

19. For discussion of the refrain, "Yahweh of Hosts is his name," see my essay entitled "YHWH Ṣebā'ôt šemô: A Form-Critical Analysis," *Zeitschrift für die alttestamentliche Wissenschaft* 81 (1969):156–75.

20. Von Rad, *The Problem of the Hexateuch*, p. 123.

21. Ibid.

22. Whenever a devotee of a particular deity came to a sacred site and slept there in quest of a vision, the practice is called incubation. In Amos 2:8 we find a reference to persons lying beside every altar upon garments taken in pledge.

23. Von Rad, *The Problem of the Hexateuch*, p. 121.

24. Ibid., p. 119. 25. Ibid., p. 113.

26. The third day functioned in ancient mythology as particularly propitious, as George M. Landes, "The 'Three Days and Three Nights' Motif in Jonah 2:1," *Journal of Biblical Literature* 86 (1976):446–50, has recognized.

27. J. J. Stamm and M. E. Andrew, *The Ten Commandments in Recent Research* (London: SCM Press, 1967), and Eduard Nielsen, *The Ten Commandments in New Perspective* (London: SCM, 1968), discuss recent interpretations of the Decalogue and offer helpful bibliography on this significant research.

28. Hermann Gunkel's pioneer work, *Schöpfung und Chaos in Urzeit und Endzeit* (Göttingen: Vandenhoeck & Ruprecht, 1895), has now been supplemented by Bernhard W. Anderson, *Creation versus Chaos* (New York: Association Press, 1967).

29. Gerhard von Rad, "The Theological Problem of the Old Testament Doctrine of Creation," in *The Problem of the Hexateuch*, pp. 131–43.

30. See my *Hymnic Affirmation of Divine Justice* (Missoula: Scholars Press, 1976), for a form critical study of the doxologies and related texts in Deutero-Isaiah and elsewhere.

31. Von Rad considered the conflict with Baalism sufficiently important to include discussion of its impact in an Old Testament the-

ology, despite a method that would seem to rule out anything but confessional statements.

32. Von Rad, *Old Testament Theology*, 1:138.

33. Ibid., pp. 154–60.   34. Ibid., p. 157.

35. God's punishment of the ancient tower builders brings back primordial chaos, thus forming an inclusio with the opening verses in Genesis. God's new departure in Gen. 12:1–3 becomes all the more urgent in this light.

36. George W. Coats, *Rebellion in the Wilderness* (Nashville: Abingdon Press, 1968), discusses the murmuring motif in the wilderness traditions of the Old Testament.

37. Neither the manna nor the quail could be stored up, except for the Sabbath.

38. Von Rad, *Old Testament Theology*, 1:311.

39. Apocalyptic has been very much in the eyes of recent critics. See especially Paul D. Hanson, *The Dawn of Apocalyptic* (Philadelphia: Fortress Press, 1975), and the July, 1977 issue of *The Catholic Biblical Quarterly*.

CHAPTER III

1. For von Rad's view of the Yahwist, see his *Old Testament Theology*, 1:136 ff., and *The Problem of the Hexateuch*, pp. 50–74.

2. Bruce Vawter, *On Genesis: A New Reading* (Garden City, N.Y.: Doubleday & Co., 1977), sums up the present state of research in this area remarkably well.

3. The law and gospel dialectic functions in von Rad's thought when least expected, often leading to profound analysis, particularly of legal texts incorporated within Deuteronomy and wisdom literature, where von Rad stresses the tension in which the sages held a belief in retribution.

4. Von Rad, *The Problem of the Hexateuch*, pp. 59, 65.

5. Although Gen. 22 has five references to Elohim and an equal number to Yahweh, the latter name occurs in fixed formulae (angel of the Lord, whisper or oracle of the Lord, and puns on the name Yahweh).

6. Considerable light has been shed upon the history of Israel in recent times. Important works include, among others, Martin Noth, *The History of Israel* (New York: Harper & Bros., 1958), John Bright, *A History of Israel*, 2nd ed., (Philadelphia: Westminster Press, 1972), and Siegfried Herrmann, *A History of Israel in Old Testament Times* (Philadelphia: Fortress Press, 1975).

7. Siegfried Herrmann, "Die konstruktive Restauration: Das Deu-

teronomium als Mitte biblischer Theologie," in *Probleme biblischer Theologie,* ed., Wolff., pp. 155–70, examines the central place Deuteronomy has played for a number of scholars.

8. Von Rad, *Old Testament Theology,* 1:231.

9. Ibid.

10. On the importance of this notion, see von Rad's essay "There Remains still a Rest for the People of God," pp. 94–102.

11. Von Rad, *Old Testament Theology,* 1:230.

12. Gerhard von Rad., "Die falschen Propheten," in *Gesammelte Studien zum Alten Testament,* 2:212–23.

13. On the other hand, the text alludes to Jehoiachin's death, a decisive argument against von Rad's understanding of the ending to the Deuteronomistic history.

14. Martin Noth's *Überlieferungsgeschichtliche Studien* (Tübingen: Max Niemeyer Verlag, 1957), is an indispensable guide to the Deuteronomistic work.

15. Von Rad, *Old Testament Theology,* 1:343, 337.

16. Ibid., pp. 232–79. Frank Moore Cross, Jr., *Canaanite Myth and Hebrew Epic* (Cambridge: Harvard University Press, 1973), has offered some suggestive comments about the essential character of the priestly document.

17. Worship in Israel ran the gamut of human response—from exuberant dancing and ecstatic excess to solemn stillness in the presence of the Holy One. Several helpful discussions have recently appeared, above all, H. J. Kraus, *Worship in Israel* (Richmond: John Knox Press, 1965); Walter Harrelson, *From Fertility Cult to Worship* (Garden City: Doubleday & Co., 1969); H. H. Rowley, *Worship in Ancient Israel* (London: SPCK, 1967).

18. Besides von Rad's earlier work, *Das Geschichtsbild des chronistischen Werkes,* see *Old Testament Theology,* 1:347–54, and "The Levitical Sermon in I and II Chronicles," in *The Problem of the Hexateuch,* pp. 267–80.

19. Von Rad, *Old Testament Theology,* 1: 354. Here von Rad cites Julius Wellhausen's comment in *Prolegomena to the History of Ancient Israel.*

20. Von Rad, *Old Testament Theology,* 1:351.

21. Ibid., vol. 2, parts one and two, have appeared in a popular version under the title, *The Message of the Prophets* (New York: Harper & Row, 1962).

22. On Bernhard Duhm's general study of the prophets, see his *Israels Propheten* (Tübingen: J. C. B. Mohr Verlag, 1922). On Jeremiah and Isaiah, consult his *Jeremia* (Tübingen: J. C. B. Mohr Verlag, 1901),

and *Das Buch Jesaja* (Göttingen: Vandenhoeck & Ruprecht, 1892).

23. Books dealing with Israelite prophecy are legion. The following works deserve special attention: Johannes Lindblom, *Prophecy in Ancient Israel* (Philadelphia: Muhlenberg Press, 1962); Abraham J. Heschel, *The Prophets* (New York: Harper & Row, 1962).

24. Several recent critics have returned to a topic that von Rad tackled quite early, and with little real depth, namely false prophecy. See Crenshaw, *Prophetic Conflict,* and Thomas W. Overholt, *The Threat of Falsehood* (London: SCM Press, 1970).

25. Heschel, *The Prophets.*

26. Sigmund Mowinckel, "The 'Spirit' and the 'Word' in the Pre-exilic Reforming Prophets," *Journal of Biblical Literature* 53 (1934): 199–227.

27. Albrecht Alt, "Das Gottesurteil auf dem Karmel," in *Kleine Schriften zur Geschichte Israels* (Munich: C. H. Beck'sche Verlagsbuchhandlung, 1953–59), pp. 270 ff.; *Essays on Old Testament History and Religion* (London: Basil Blackwell, 1966).

28. Sheldon Blank, *Prophetic Faith in Isaiah* (London: Adam and Charles Black, 1958), distinguishes Isaiah of fact from the legendary prophet depicted in these chapters.

29. His assumption is that women necessarily become ritually unclean, and would therefore jeopardize all sacred activity in a cultic center.

30. Sigmund Mowinckel, *Prophecy and Tradition* (Oslo: I Kommisjon Hos Jacob Dybwad, 1946).

31. M. P. Matheney, Jr., "Interpretation of Hebrew Prophetic Symbolic Act," *Encounter* 29 (1968): 256–63, brings H. Wheeler Robinson's study of prophetic symbolism up to date ("Prophetic Symbolism," in *Old Testament Essays,* ed. Th. H. Robinson, [London: Charles Griffin and Company, Ltd., 1927] pp. 1–17).

32. For the recent debate, see H. H. Rowley, "The Marriage of Hosea," in *Men of God* (London: Thomas Nelson & Sons, 1963), and I. H. Eybers, "The Matrimonial Life of Hosea," in *Studies on the Books of Hosea and Amos,* ed. A. H. van Zyl, *Die Ou Testamentiese Werkgemeenshap in Suid-Afrika,* (Potchefstroom: Pro Rega-Pers Beperk, 1964–65).

33. Brevard S. Childs, *Isaiah and the Assyrian Crisis* (London: SCM Press, 1967), offers a form critical analysis of the texts dealing with this crisis.

34. G. Henton Davies, "Gerhard von Rad, Old Testament Theology," in *Contemporary Old Testament Theologians,* ed. Robert B. Laurin (Valley Forge: Judson Press, 1970), pp. 79–80.

35. In addition to the works on apocalyptic previously referred to, two books merit attention: H. H. Rowley, *The Relevance of Apocalyptic* (London: Lutterworth Press, 1944), and D. S. Russell, *The Method and Message of Jewish Apocalyptic* (Philadelphia: Westminster Press, 1964).

36. Von Rad's early venture into this difficult terrain, though remarkably suggestive, hardly stands on the same level with *Wisdom in Israel* (see *Old Testament Theology*, 1:418–59). On the phrase, "Die Antwort Israels," see Christoph Barth in *Probleme biblischer Theologie*, Wolff, ed., pp. 44–56.

37. Among the many books on wisdom, the following represent the status of research. James L. Crenshaw, *Studies in Ancient Israelite Wisdom* (New York: Ktav Publishing House, 1976), J. Coert Rylaarsdam, *Revelation in Jewish Wisdom Literature* (Chicago: The University of Chicago Press, 1946); R. B. Y. Scott, *The Way of Wisdom in the Old Testament* (New York: Macmillan, 1971).

38. Brian W. Kovacs, "Is There a Class-Ethic in Proverbs?" in *Essays in Old Testament Ethics*, ed. James L. Crenshaw and John T. Willis (New York: Ktav Publishing House, 1974), 171–89, answers his question positively.

39. Robert Gordis, "The Social Background of Wisdom Literature," *Hebrew Union College Annual* 18 (1943/44):77–118, reaches a similar conclusion.

40. On wisdom forms see my essay, "Wisdom," in *Old Testament Form Criticism*, ed. John H. Hayes (San Antonio: Trinity University Press, 1974), 225–64.

41. I have given an extensive critique of von Rad's interpretation of wisdom in "*Wisdom in Israel*, By Gerhard von Rad," *Religious Studies Review* 2/2 (1976):6–12.

42. Walter Harrelson, "Wisdom and Pastoral Theology," *Andover Newton Quarterly* (1966), pp. 3–11, writes that such modern attempts to master life carry the wisdom tradition into the present age.

43. Here von Rad relies upon an important study by Walther Zimmerli. See Zimmerli, "The Place and Limit of the Wisdom in the Framework of the Old Testament Theology," in *Studies in Ancient Israelite Wisdom*, ed. Crenshaw, pp. 314–26.

44. Gerhard von Rad, "Weisheit und Geschichte," in *Probleme biblischer Theologie*, ed. Wolff., 136–54.

45. Johannes Fichtner, *Die altorientalische Weisheit in ihrer israelitisch-jüdischen Ausprägung*, Beihefte zur Zeitschrift für die alttestamentliche Wissenschaft, vol. 62 (Giessen: Alfred Töpelmann Verlag, 1933).

46. For my reasons, see my article "Method in Determining Wisdom

Influence upon 'Historical' Literature," *Journal of Biblical Literature* 88 (1969) : 129–42.

47. H. D. Preuss, "Erwägungen zum theologischen Ort alttestament-licher Weisheitsliteratur," *Evangelische Theologie* 30 (1970) :393–417, reaches extreme conclusions along this line. For him wisdom is pa-ganism.

48. Perhaps the most devastating blow to salvation history as uniquely Israelite came from Bertil Albrektson's *History and the Gods* (Lund: C. W. K. Gleerup, 1967). Von Rad did not seem to grasp the impact of this work.

49. Rylaarsdam devotes considerable discussion to the emergence of the idea of grace within wisdom, and associates this phenomenon with loss of self confidence.

50. Two persons in particular have been active on the American scene: Walter Brueggemann (*In Man We Trust* [Richmond: John Knox, 1972]), and Roland Murphy, whose essays in various journals have covered a wide range of subjects in Israelite wisdom.

CHAPTER IV

1. Von Rad's little book, *Moses*, demonstrates amazing skill in the art of popularizing the results of biblical scholarship.

2. Radically different interpretations appear in Dewey M. Beegle, *Moses, the Servant of Yahweh* (Grand Rapids: Wm. B. Eerdmans, 1972) ; Sigmund Freud, *Moses and Monotheism* (New York: Vintage, 1939) ; and Martin Buber, *Moses* (New York: Harper and Bros., 1946).

3. Von Rad, *Moses*, p. 8.   4. Ibid., p. 15.   5. Ibid., p. 16.

6. Albrecht Alt, "The Origins of Israelite Law," in *Essays on Old Testament History and Religion*, ed. Crenshaw and Willis, (Oxford: Basil Blackwell, 1966), 79–132.

7. Martin Noth, *The Laws in the Pentateuch* (London: Oliver and Boyd), 1966, constitutes a thorough study of Israelite law.

8. Ludwig Koehler, *Hebrew Man* (Nashville: Abingdon, 1956).

9. The Hebrew word may be translated either passive or reflexive. The former rendering makes Abraham a means of blessing, and the latter implies that people pronounce a formula like "May God bless you as he blessed Abraham."

10. Von Rad, *Moses*, p. 79.

11. Von Rad seems constrained to see Christian significance for Old Testament texts, a tendency that seems to be gaining impetus today in several circles. I have grave doubts about the legitimacy of such a pro-cedure.

12. Von Rad's *Das Opfer des Abraham* focuses upon Abraham's supreme sacrifice, thus avoiding the ambiguity inherent within "the sacrifice of Isaac," where Isaac can be either subject or object of the action.

13. I have attempted to understand this story from the standpoint of aesthetic criticism in "Journey into Oblivion: A Structural Analysis of Gen. 22:1–19," *Soundings* 58 (1975):243–56.

14. Erich Auerbach, *Mimesis* (Princeton: Princeton University Press, 1953), pp. 3–23.

15. Shalom Spiegel, *The Last Trial* (New York: Schocken Books, 1967), offers a profound discussion of Jewish reflection on the actual sacrifice of Isaac.

16. In the Hebrew, only Abraham returns to his servants, who then accompany him to Beersheba. The strange silence about Isaac's conduct after the ordeal suggested to some rabbis that Abraham may have in fact offered his son, but that a new ending has been attached to the story. In "Typological Interpretation of the Old Testament," von Rad writes: "he who had been laid by his father on God's altar carried the secret of his life with him to the grave" (p. 29).

17. The tension between God who reveals himself and the hidden God already occurs in the Old Testament. Theologians and mystics have simply underscored an authentic biblical understanding of God.

18. Von Rad, *Das Opfer des Abraham*. He discusses Luther's comments on pp. 45–57. Sören Kierkegaard's treatment (from *Fear and Trembling* [Garden City, N.Y.: Doubleday & Co., 1941], pp. 26–37), is discussed on pp. 58–80. Kolakowski's powerful satire, discussed on pp. 82–85, ought to be taken with utmost seriousness by those who wish to understand the text. Von Rad discusses Rembrandt's art on pp. 86–95. The impact of Rembrandt's quite different ways of viewing the story is unforgettable. In this case, a picture is truly worth a thousand words.

19. Hermann Gunkel, *Genesis* (Göttingen: Vandenhoeck Ruprecht, 1901), p. 237.

20. Jewish tradition reports that Isaac died on the altar, and God restored him to life in the garden of Eden.

21. Shalom Spiegel, *The Last Trial*.

22. Gerhard von Rad, "The Joseph Narrative and Ancient Wisdom," in *The Problem of the Hexateuch*, pp. 292–300; *Die Josephgeschichte* (Neukirchen: Kreis Moers, 1954); "Biblische Joseph-Erzählung und Joseph-Roman," *Neue Rundschau* 76 (1965): 546–59.

23. Von Rad, *The Problem of the Hexateuch*, p. 293.

24. Von Rad, *Die Josephgeschichte*, p. 7.

25. For current research on Ecclesiastes, see my essay, "The Eternal Gospel (Eccl. 3:11)," in *Essays in Old Testament Ethics,* ed. Crenshaw and Willis, pp. 23–55.

26. Von Rad *The Problem of the Hexateuch,* p. 296.

27. Ibid., p. 297.

28. For a challenge to von Rad's understanding of the Joseph story, see my "Method in Determining Wisdom Influence upon 'Historical' Literature," *Journal of Biblical Literature* 88 (1969):129–42. George Coats, "The Joseph Story and Ancient Wisdom: A Reappraisal," *Catholic Biblical Quarterly* 35 (1973):285–97, and *From Canaan to Egypt,* Monograph, no. 4, Catholic Biblical Quarterly, Washington, D.C.: 1976, takes a mediating position in the debate.

29. Gerhard von Rad, "The Beginnings of Historical Writing in Ancient Israel," in *The Problem of the Hexateuch,* pp. 166–204; *Old Testament Theology,* 1:308–326.

30. Von Rad, *The Problem of the Hexateuch,* p. 190.

31. Leonhard Rost, *Das Kleine Credo und andere Studien zum Alten Testament* (Heidelberg: Quelle und Meyer, 1965).

32. Von Rad, *The Problem of the Hexateuch,* p. 170.

33. These Israelite sagas have been neglected for too long. I have recently studied the Samson saga from the standpoint of aesthetic criticism. This volume, *Samson, A Secret Betrayed, A Vow Ignored,* will be published by John Knox Press in 1978.

34. Von Rad, *Old Testament Theology,* 1:313.

35. Von Rad, *The Problem of the Hexateuch,* p. 187.

36. Ibid., p. 201.

37. Von Rad, *Old Testament Theology,* 1:316–17.

38. Ibid., 318.

39. Von Rad, *Old Testament Theology,* 2:188–219; "Die Konfessionen Jeremias," *Evangelische Theologie* 3 (1936):265–76.

40. Sheldon Blank: "The Prophet as Paradigm," *Essays in Old Testament Ethics,* ed. Crenshaw and Willis, pp. 111–30.

41. Von Rad, *Old Testament Theology,* 2:204.

42. Ibid., p. 206.   43. Ibid., p. 203.   44. Ibid., p. 204.
45. Ibid., p. 208.   46. Ibid., p. 207.   47. Ibid., p. 219.

CHAPTER V

1. Gerhard von Rad, "Some Aspects of the Old Testament World View," in *The Problem of the Hexateuch,* p. 144.

2. Part one of *Wisdom in Israel* concerns the centers and transmitters of didactic traditions and literary forms. The second part treats the

liberation of reason and the resultant problems, while part three takes up various topics of special interest, especially creation's self-revelation and the dialectic of trust and attack.

3. Zimmerli, "The Place and Limit of the Wisdom in the Framework of the Old Testament Theology."

4. Preuss, "Erwägungen zum theologischen Ort alttestamentlicher Weisheitsliteratur."

5. Hans Heinrich Schmid, "Schöpfung, Gerechtigkeit und Heil: Schöpfungstheologie als Gesamthorizont biblischer Theologie," *Zeitschrift für Theologie und Kirche* 70 (1973):1–19.

6. James L. Crenshaw, *Studies in Ancient Israelite Wisdom*, pp. 26–35, 43–45.

7. Von Rad, *The Problem of the Hexateuch*, p. 147.

8. Ibid., p. 149.   9. Ibid., p. 164.   10. Ibid., p. 154.

11. Two texts stand out as significant in this regard: Gen. 18 and Judges 6:11–24.

12. David Neiman, *The Book of Job* (Jerusalem: Massada, 1972), uses this language to refer to human self-centeredness.

13. Von Rad, *The Problem of the Hexateuch*, p. 152.

14. Ibid., p. 151.

15. Von Rad, *Wisdom in Israel*, p. 169.

16. Leo G. Perdue, *Wisdom and Cult*, SBL Dissertation Series 30 (Missoula: Scholars Press, 1977).

17. See also Hartmut Gese, "Die Krisis der Weisheit bei Kohelet," *Les sagesses du Proché-Orient ancien* (Paris: Presses Universitaires de France, 1963), pp. 139–51.

18. Walther Zimmerli, *The Law and the Prophets* (Oxford: Basil Blackwell, 1965); *Man and His Hope in the Old Testament* (London: SCM Press, 1970).

19. Gerhard von Rad, "Gerichtsdoxologie," *Schalom: Studien zu Glaube und Geschichte Israels*, edited by Karl-Heinz Bernhardt (Stuttgart: Calwer Verlag, 1971), pp. 28–37. His last essay was entitled "Beobachtungen an der Moseerzählung Ex. 1–14," *Evangelische Theologie* 31 (1971):579–88.

20. Friedrich Horst, "Die Doxologien im Amosbuch," in *Gottes Recht* (Munich: Chr. Kaiser Verlag, 1961), pp. 155–66.

21. James L. Crenshaw, "The Problem of Theodicy in Sirach," *Journal of Biblical Literature* 94 (1975):47–64.

22. This discussion of theodicy originally appeared in the Festschrift to Otto Procksch in 1934, pp. 45–70.

23. Peter von der Osten-Sacken, *Die Apokalyptik in ihrem Verhältnis zu Prophetie und Weisheit* (Munich: Chr. Kaiser Verlag, 1969).

CHAPTER VI

1. See von Rad, *Old Testament Theology*, vol. 2, part three.
2. See M. Jack Suggs, *Wisdom, Christology and Law in Matthew's Gospel* (Cambridge: Harvard University Press, 1970).
3. Von Rad, *Old Testament Theology*, 2:375.
4. Gerhard von Rad, "Typological Interpretation of the Old Testament," in *Essays on Old Testament Hermeneutics*, ed. Claus Westermann (Richmond: John Knox Press, 1963), pp. 17–39. Von Rad describes Israel's typological thinking as an eschatological correspondence between beginning and end, emphasizes the Old Testament as a history book, and writes that "the 'tradition' is so zealous for God that the event is straightway broadened into the typical" (p. 34). He concludes: "One must therefore . . . really speak of a witness of the Old Testament to Christ . . . Christ is given to us only through the double witness of those who await and those who remember" (p. 39). For expansion of typological exegesis along lines approved by von Rad, see H. W. Wolff, *Gesammelten Studien zum Alten Testament* (Munich: Chr. Kaiser Verlag, 1973), pp. 251–88 and 325–44.
5. Hans Walter Wolff writes that a moment of meditation set in ("Gespräch mit Gerhard von Rad," p. 657), and Karl Rahner thinks of divine silence as a reward for faithful listening to the text ("Gerhard von Rad," p. 10). On the other hand, M. E. Andrew observes that von Rad was perhaps overcome by sadness as a result of restlessness among theologians in his later years ("Gerhard von Rad—A Personal Memoir," p. 300).

CHAPTER VII

1. Klaus Koch, "Gerhard von Rad," in *Tendenzen der Theologie in 20. Jahrhundert: Eine Geschichte in Porträts*, ed. H. J. Schultz, 1966, p. 483.
2. This sense of nationalistic consciousness reaches a significant peak in *The Old Testament—God's Word for the Germans!*
3. Koch, "Gerhard von Rad," p. 483.
4. Hermann Gunkel, *What Remains of the Old Testament* (New York: The Macmillan Company, 1928). Besides the essay on what is left of the Old Testament when critics finish their task, other articles in this book concern fundamental problems of Hebrew literary history, the religion of the Psalms, the ending in Micah, and Jacob.
5. Wolfhart Pannenberg, ed., *Revelation as History* (New York: Macmillan, 1968).

6. On the problem of actualizing traditions in Israel, see Peter R. Ackroyd, "Continuity and Discontinuity: Rehabilitation and Authentication" in *Tradition and Theology in the Old Testament*, ed. Douglas A. Knight (Philadelphia: Fortress Press, 1977), pp. 215–34, and my essay, "The Human Dilemma and Literature of Dissent," in *ibid.*, pp. 235–58.

7. Wolfhart Pannenberg, "Glaube und Wirklichkeit im Denken Gerhard von Rads," in *Gerhard von Rad: Seine Bedeutung für die Theologie*, pp. 37–54, 57–58, examines this facet of von Rad's volume on wisdom.

8. Friedrich Baumgärtel, "Gerhard von Rads 'Theologie des Alten Testaments,' " pp. 812–13. In this caustic attack on von Rad, Baumgärtel observes that Nathan Söderblom, a historian of religion, had already in 1931 proposed the outline von Rad later arrived at, and that Van der Leeuw recognized (in 1933) the phenomenon of ever new interpretations of saving facts which was by no means unique to Israel.

9. Martin Honecker, "Zum Verständnis der Geschichte in Gerhard von Rads Theologie des Alten Testaments," *Evangelische Theologie* 23 (1963):143–168. See also the somewhat intemperate assessment by D. G. Spriggs, *Two Old Testament Theologies*, pp. 34–59.

10. Above all, see Hyatt, "Were There an Ancient Historical Credo in Israel and an Independent Sinai Tradition?"

11. Martin Honecker, "Zum Verständnis der Geschichte in Gerhard von Rads Theologie des Alten Testaments," pp. 143–48.

12. Siegfried Herrmann, "Die Konstruktive Restauration: Das Deuteronomium als Mitte biblischer Theologie," in *Probleme biblischer Theologie*, pp. 155–70.

13. G. Henton Davies, "Gerhard von Rad," p. 79.

14. Wolff, "Gespräch mit Gerhard von Rad," p. 648.

15. Davies, "Gerhard von Rad," p. 80.

Selected Bibliography

WORKS BY GERHARD VON RAD

A complete listing of von Rad's publications appears in Rolf Rendtorff and Klaus Koch, eds., *Studien zur Theologie der altestamentlichen Überlieferungen*, pp. 163–74, and H. W. Wolff, ed., *Probleme biblischer Theologie*, pp. 665–81. Konrad von Rabenau prepared the bibliography through 1970.

"Ancient Word and Living Word. The Preaching of Deuteronomy and Our Preaching." *Interpretation* 15 (1961):3–13.

"Antrittsrede von Gerhard von Rad." (Inaugural address of Gerhard von Rad as member of the Heidelberg Academy of Science.) Sitzungsberichte der Heidelberger Akademie der Wissenschaften, 1955/56, 1957, pp. 24–36.

"Antwort auf Conzelmanns Fragen," *Evangelische Theologie* 14 (1964): 388–94.

Biblical Interpretations in Preaching. Translated by John E. Steely. Nashville: Abingdon Press, 1977.

"Biblische Joseph-Erzählung und Joseph-Roman." *Neue Rundschau* 76 (1965):546–59.

Deuteronomy. Philadelphia: The Westminster Press, 1966.

Erinnerungen aus der Kriegsgefangenschaft Frühjahr 1945. Neukirchen-Vluyn: Neukirchener Verlag, 1976.

Genesis. Translated by John H. Marks. Philadelphia: The Westminster Press, 1972. Revised edition, 1976.

Gesammelte Studien zum Alten Testament. Vol. 1. Theologische Bücherei, vol. 8. Munich: Chr. Kaiser Verlag, 1961.

Gesammelte Studien zum Alten Testament. Vol. 2. Theologische Bücherei, vol. 48. Edited by Rudolf Smend. Munich: Chr. Kaiser Verlag, 1973.

Das Geschichtsbild des chronistischen Werkes. Beiträge zur Wissenschaft vom Alten und Neuen Testament, vol. 54. Stuttgart: W. Kohlhammer Verlag, 1930.

Das Gottesvolk im Deuteronomium. Beiträge zur Wissenschaft vom Alten und Neuen Testament, vol. 47. Stuttgart: W. Kohlhammer Verlag, 1929.

Gottes Wirken im Israel. Edited by Odil Hannes Steck. Neukirchen-Vluyn: Neukirchener Verlag, 1974.

Der Heilige Krieg im alten Israel. Rev. ed. Göttingen: Vandenhoeck & Ruprecht, 1958.

Die Josephgeschichte. Neukirchen: Kreis Moers. 1954.

"Man and the Guidance of the Hidden God in the Old Testament." *The Student World* 44 (1951) :140–47.

The Message of the Prophets. New York: Harper & Row, 1962.

Moses. London: Lutterworth Press, 1960.

Old Testament Theology. 2 vols. New York: Harper & Row, 1962, 1965.

Das Opfer des Abraham. Munich: Chr. Kaiser Verlag, 1971.

"The Origin of the Concept of the Day of Yahweh." *Journal of Semitic Studies* 4 (1959) :97–108.

Predigten. Edited by Ursula von Rad. Munich. Chr. Kaiser Verlag, 1972.

The Problem of the Hexateuch and Other Essays. Translated by E. W. Trueman Dicken. Edinburgh and London: Oliver and Boyd, 1965; New York: McGraw-Hill, 1966.

Studies in Deuteronomy. Translated by David Stalker. London: SCM Press, 1953.

"Typological Interpretation of the Old Testament." In *Essays on Old Testament Hermeneutics,* edited by Claus Westermann. Richmond: John Knox Press, 1969, pp. 17–39.

"Über Gerhard von Rad." In *Probleme biblischer Theologie,* edited by Hans Walter Wolff, pp. 659–61.

Wisdom in Israel. Translated by James D. Martin. London: SCM Press, 1972; Nashville: Abingdon Press, 1973.

WORKS ABOUT GERHARD VON RAD

Andrew, M. E. "Gerhard von Rad—A Personal Memoir." *Expository Times* 83 (1972) :296–300.

Baumgärtel, Friedrich. "Gerhard von Rads 'Theologie des Alten Testaments.' " *Theologische Literaturzeitung* 86 (1961) :801–815, 895–907.

Clements, Ronald E. *One Hundred Years of Old Testament Interpretation.* Philadelphia: The Westminster Press, 1976.

Conzelmann, Hans. "Fragen an Gerhard von Rad." *Evangelische Theologie* 24 (1964):113–25.

Crenshaw, James L. "Wisdom in Israel, by Gerhard von Rad." *Religious Studies Review* 22 (1976):6–12.

Davies, G. Henton. "Gerhard von Rad, 'Old Testament Theology.'" In *Contemporary Old Testament Theologians,* edited by Robert B. Laurin. Valley Forge: Judson Press, 1970, pp. 63–89.

Honecker, Martin. "Zum Verständnis der Geschichte in Gerhard von Rads Theologie des Alten Testaments." *Evangelische Theologie* 23 (1963):143–68.

Hyatt, J. Philip. "Were There an Ancient Historical Credo in Israel and an Independent Sinai Tradition?" In *Translating and Understanding the Old Testament,* edited by H. T. Frank and W. L. Reed. Nashville: Abingdon Press, 1970, pp. 152–70.

Koch, Klaus. "Gerhard von Rad." In *Tendenzen der Theologie in 20 Jahrhundert: Eine Geschichte in Porträts,* edited by H. J. Schultz. Stuttgart & Berlin: Kreuz Verlag, 1966, pp. 483–87.

Rahner, Karl. "Gerhard von Rad." *Das Parlament* 35 (Aug. 26, 1972):10.

Rendtorff, Rolf and Koch, Klaus, eds. *Studien zur Theologie der alttestamentlichen Überlieferungen.* Neukirchen: Neukirchener Verlag, 1961.

Schmidt, W. H. " 'Theologie des Alten Testaments' vor und nach Gerhard von Rad." In *Verkündigung und Forschung.* Beihefte zu 'Evangelische Theologie' Altes Testament, vol. 1. Munich: Chr. Kaiser Verlag, 1972, pp. 1–25.

Spriggs, D. G. *Two Old Testament Theologies.* Studies in Biblical Theology, 2nd Series, vol. 30. Naperville, Ill.: Alec R. Allenson, Inc., 1974.

Timm, H. " 'Das weite Herz.' Religiöses Philosophieren in Israel. Zu Gerhard von Rads Weisheits-Buch," *Zeitschrift für Theologie und Kirche* 74 (1977): 224–37.

Wolff, Hans Walter. "Gespräch mit Gerhard von Rad." In *Probleme Biblischer Theologie,* edited by Hans Walter Wolff, pp. 648–58.

Wolff, Hans Walter, ed. *Probleme biblischer Theologie: Gerhard von Rad zum 70 Geburtstag.* Munich: Chr. Kaiser Verlag, 1971.

Wolff, H. W., Rendtorff, Rolf, and Pannenberg, Wolfhart, eds. *Gerhard von Rad: Seine Bedeutung für die Theologie.* Munich: Chr. Kaiser Verlag, 1973.

Zimmerli, Walther. "Gerhard von Rad, 'Theologie des Alten Testaments.'" *Vetus Testamentum* 13 (1963):100–111.

————. "Die Weisheit Israels: Zu einem Buch von Gerhard von Rad." *Evangelische Theologie* 31 (1971):680–95.